The Civil War Letters
✯✯ of ✯✯
William A. Robinson

AND THE STORY OF THE
89TH NEW YORK VOLUNTEER INFANTRY

Robert J. Taylor

HERITAGE BOOKS
2011

HERITAGE BOOKS
AN IMPRINT OF HERITAGE BOOKS, INC.

Books, CDs, and more—Worldwide

For our listing of thousands of titles see our website at
www.HeritageBooks.com

Published 2011 by
HERITAGE BOOKS, INC.
Publishing Division
100 Railroad Ave. #104
Westminster, Maryland 21157

Copyright © 2000 Robert J. Taylor

All rights reserved. No part of this book may be reproduced or transmitted in any form or by any means, electronic or mechanical, including photocopying, recording or by any information storage and retrieval system without written permission from the author, except for the inclusion of brief quotations in a review.

International Standard Book Numbers
Paperbound: 978-0-7884-1580-7
Clothbound: 978-0-7884-8874-0

The Civil War Letters of William A. Robinson And The Story of the Eighty Ninth New York Volunteer Infantry

INTRODUCTION

In the summer of 1861 in various towns and cities in New York, the call was going out for volunteers to fight for the preservation of the Union. The plea was not lost on the central New York farm folk of rural Delaware County. One of the men who stepped forward was a married father of two young sons and who was one of my great, great grandfathers. He was a tall, lanky, resourceful, and pious man. He was one of the region's common men, a farmer, a descendant of generations of American farmers. His family also had a strong history of volunteerism when the Nation had a need. His father and both of his father's brothers were veterans of the War of 1812. His father's father and both of his wife's grandfathers were veterans of the Revolutionary War. Whether or not this history played a role in his enlistment is unknown, but it is reasonable to suspect that it did.

When William reported for duty and was mustered into Company I of the Eighty Ninth New York Volunteer Infantry in the fall of 1861, he left behind his wife and two children, but resolved not to lose touch with his family. He endeavored to write regularly to his wife, to his sisters and brother, and to his mother. It was my great fortune to find that about 115 of his letters to his wife, Mary, had survived to the present in good condition. Through the generosity and trust of the possessor of the originals, I was lent the letters for about one year. They had not been catalogued, and in some cases had portions mixed up with letters of other dates. These were carefully returned to the best estimate of actual timings and proper page combinations.

A remarkable treasure of family information unfolded during the reading and transcription of those letters, but it became abundantly clear that there was a wealth of other information contained therein. The military unit that William served in has had scant literary record published. I was sure that the letters, and the bits of information sprinkled among the family notes and accountings of the enlisted man's life in the service, sometimes routine and sometimes not, could be of value in fleshing out the knowledge of activities of the Eighty Ninth New York Volunteers. When I found that there were notations of wounds, disease and deaths among his comrades, seemingly nowhere else to be found, it was also clear that other people might find longed for information in the dissemination of the writings. And, once again, it might be possible to relive the conditions of the Northern foot soldier in the thought and word of an actual participant. So, with these things in mind, I have attempted to put these letters, together with some explanations and historical notations into the public forum.

Each letter is transcribed faithfully as it was written, that is with its attendant spelling and misspelling, capitalization and punctuation. The urge to embellish or 'explain' a letter had to be suppressed and is left to the reader to add or discern any special meaning. A few explanatory notes are added as footnotes.

Finally, a historical picture of the Eighty Ninth New York Volunteer Regiment and some tables of informaton about the men in the unit has been presented to correlate with the letter transcriptions.

Robert J. Taylor, M.D.

William A. Robinson

William was born in Sing Sing (now Ossining), Westchester County, New York on February 24, 1831, as the seventh of a total of nine children of Alfred Robinson and his wife Sarah Elizabeth (Smith) Robinson. He grew up largely in Delaware County, New York. He and Mary were married in Hobart, Delaware Co., New York on April 19, 1858. Before and after the War of the Rebellion, he was sometimes a mason, sometimes a farmer, and sometimes worked as a tinker or laborer. He died September 27, 1911 in the Town of Kortright, Delaware Co., New York and is buried in the Sackrider Cemetery in that town.

Mary E. (Sackrider) Robinson

Mary E. Sackrider was born September 18, 1838 in the Town of Kortright, Delaware Co., New York to Timothy Sackrider and his wife Nancy (Goodenough) Sackrider as the fourth of seven children. Before the war began, she delivered two boys, Charles, born 1859, and Daniel, born 1860, whom she cared for through the three years of her husband's absence. After the war, she had three more children. Mary died July 15, 1920 at a son's home and is buried with her husband in the Sackrider Cemetery.

The Civil War Letters of William A. Robinson
And
The Story of the Eighty Ninth New York Volunteer Infantry

Table of Contents

Introduction	page 1
William A. Robinson	page 3
Mary E. (Sackrider) Robinson	page 4

Letter Transcriptions -

Chapter One - 1861, 1862	page 6
Chapter Two - 1863	page 52
Chapter Three - 1864	page 86

Chapter Four - A History of the Eighty Ninth New York Volunteer Infantry	page 117
Colonel Harrison Fairchild	page 145
Appendix A - Military Service of the Men of Company I	page 147
Appendix B – Regimental Staff Officers	page 160
Appendix C - Rosters of Companies A through H, and K	page 163
Appendix D - Compiled List of Men Crossing the Rappahanock River December 11, 1862	page 184
Bibliography	page 187
Index	page 188

Chapter One
Letter Transcriptions 1861 and 1862

Oct 18   This short letter is written on a half sheet of lined, commemorative paper. The heading is: Elmira   On the obverse is a lady with an American Flag in red, white and blue, and written on this side is Mary E. Robinson $4,00. On the reverse is the note:

Dar wif

    We arived hear about noon yesterday safe and well   we ar all in good spirits   I shall write the first of the week   til then I remain your afectionat Husband

                        W A Robinson

Nov 21st /61   This letter is on blue, lined paper which is embossed in the upper left corner. It is headed: Camp Leslie

Dear
    Mary   I am well and harty and hope this will find you the same   I have wated to get money   I cannot get any of the Captain but have had good luck borrowing to send for books and am reding as fast as I can get them   I have the promis of $10,00 in about a week   then I can send you as much as you will want   it may be a month yet before we get pay   I sen you $1,00   I dar not send any more as I have to pay in a day or tow what I have borrowed and want a little to send for more books   I think we shall move from hear in about 2 weeks   send a leter by W Halsted[1] when he comes

and let me know what you nead and if I cannot get enough with out I will write to Delhi where I can get it   yours in hast
        and yours for ever
             W A Robinson

Nov. 28th /61   This is headed: Camp Leslie

Dear Mary

---
[1] William Halstead, Pvt. Co. I

I agane adress you   I recived a leter from you the same day I sent the last and look for another to day   we have had a hard time hear with the measles but ar well or getting beter   I do not think ther is any left in camp that is catching   we lost one boy last sunday in the hospital with inflamation on the lungs   it was Wesley Epps of Franklin   I watched

with him Saturday and sunday and laid him out and com back to camp & found about 20 sick in our bunch and went to nursing them   I had quite a bad head ache yesterday but feels much beter to day   I shall report for duty to morow   there is only 3 that neads waiting on hear now   William Becker is one of them   there is one more at a private house   he is giting beter and 4 at the hospital   they are so as to go out doors   we have orders to march to morow but will not start till next week

you must not write till you hear from me agane   I expect some money the last of the week   as soon as I get it I shall write agane Wee will get our pay as soon as we get to the land of coton Cormack[2] is coming home   I shall send my carpet bag and some under cloths   you can get it by sending to Englands store   I shall keep the rest   I found that said shirt last night   our camp equipage has com and we get muskets instid of rifles and some of the boys are mad about that

but if we can only get to a new place it is all I care for at present for I have got tired of looking at these hills though I am as comfortable here as I could hope to be in any place   but I want a change either for the beter or wors   I shall be home again in the spring and feel shure it will be for good   keep up good spirits and do you best bing shure that God will order all things for the good of those that put there trust in him   and now good by for the present and God bless you and the children

William Robinson

Dec 5th 1861 This letter is headed: Camp Leslie

Dear Mary

                      I heard

---

[2] Lt. Robert Cormack, of Co. I

yesterday that you was sick   had we been going to stay hear a week I should have come home but we start for Dixy to day and when you get this I shall be in a warmer climate   I have been in a great hurry to be off but when it came I would have given a great deal for one week respite

but I supose it is all for the best   I wrote to Delhi yesterday for money and feel shure you will get some   I send $3,00   it is all I could get and will not have to thank England[3] for it neather   I think England will stoop to as mean lies to gain his ends as any man I ever saw but he must look out for me or he will remember me in a way not pleasant   we have just filed one

Company and will elect our small officers to day   I have no hope for the Captain apoints them and he has plenty of pits (?) and he has got all of me that he expects   I shall write as soon as I get in one place and you muss let me know how you are   Write as soon as you get this and direct

       Dickinson guard
       care Capt England
       Washington and
if it gets lost let it go

but I must stop for want of time   from your lovin husband
                                   W. A. Robinson

Dec 12th 61/   This letter is on lined, folded stationary with the upper left corner embossed apparently with the Latin word quoque. It is headed: Washington

Dear Mary
          I agane adress you   I sent a leter to you the day before I left Elmira with $3,00 in it   I have not heard from you in a long time   Mrs Whitney wrote that you had the measles and I am ancious to hear from home   I expect my pay the 29th of this month I have been trying to get a furlo but cannot or I should have writen 3 days ago   I am well and would be glad to think that you was   if you cannot write get some one as soon as you get this

---

[3] Theophilus England, Captain of Co. I

and let me know how you are situated   I have no hopes of getting home agane till march but after we get our pay once we shall get it every month   I have been elected corporal but do not feel very proud of it after what I have done and been promised   we are very pleasantly situated in sight of the capitol and white house   we all sleepe on the same bed with plenty of straw and blankets   I should feel contented and hapy if all was right at home but as it is I canot sleep nights or rest days

but I feel that this will be over soon and while it lasts I shall trust in god that all shall be for the best   without this trust I fel that I should be miserable indead   I like the tents and ground bed beter than I did the barocks   I think we can be comfortable with less blankets and the same weather   the weather was very mild when we got hear but it frose ice last night and an over coat feels good to day   our rigement came on two trains and they had a colision on one of them

but I was on the other   there was no one hurt to speake of   one car was stove up that Bob[4] was on and he had large stories to tell about it but I canot write any more at present   direct to
    Washington DC 89 Rigiment
    NY Volunteers
    Care Capt England
and now good by fore the present and god bless you and the children
        William A Robinson

Dec. 22, 1861 This letter is headed: Camp Clay, Co I of 89th It is written on U.S. Capitol commemorative paper.

Dear Mary
    I agane adress you   I am well an harty and would be glad to know this would find you the same   I recived yours last night   it took a lode off my mind   I can tell you we will get our pay the first of the month and I shall send you enough to last you till I can get more   we expect to get pay from the 17th

of Sept which will give me over $45,00 but they may keep one month pay back   they have had several fights lately and had good success and the talk is hear that the war will end by the first of may so keep corage   if you have hard times now it will be all for the best in the

---

[4] Robert Zeh, Pvt. Co. I

end   you nead not wory about me   I am as comfortable as I was at home and free from them aches and pane that I have had 2 winters before   the weather is fine   we have not had a storm cince we got hear   I like the life beter than I expected   I shall write to Penfield to day

and Andrews as soon as I get money   we was got up in the night last night to see how quick we could get around   the rigiment was formed in 20 minutes from the time the drum first beat   I was to the city friday   went all through the capitol and went to see Fitches Co saw Dible[5] and all the rest   we get visits from some of them every day   A B Douglass of Andes is hear to day   all the news I can get goes to show a speedy close to the war   they had a great fire in Charlstown suposed to be the work of slaves

the slaves are rising all over the south   in one batle 400 routed 1500 which shows that the southern solgers are sick of the war   I have no more at present so now good by and may God bless you and the Children and keep you for I leave you in his care knowing that his protection is beter than mine and I fel that the has had care over you since I left and I fel that we shall meat gean soon on earth but if not may we meet in heaven
From you loving husban
        W A Robinson

Dec. 28th 1861 This letter is headed: Camp Clay Co. I, 89

Dar Mary   I agane wright a line to you   I looked in vain for news from you yesterday   I recived one last week   I want you to wright as often as you can   I recived a leter from Thomas[6] cince I was hear Mother[7] was their   all was well   he sed he was much surprised to hear that I was in

the servis   I am well and harty as I ever was in my life and fare beter than I expected   wee will get our pay saturday or Monday the 3d or 5th of Jan cirtain and the day I get it I will start some home   I for got to tell you where my Carpet bag was   It was at Englands   I asked

---

[5] These probably refer to Capt. Butler Fitch, 8th Ind. NY Batt. and Pvt. Wm. Dibble of the same company.
[6] Thomas Robinson, older brother of Wm.
[7] Sarah (Smith) Robinson, mother of Wm.

Penfield to take it to Hunts and let him send it up   I hope you have got it be fore now   I have no news to write   we have not got our arms yet I and no hopes of getting them and as long

as they do not come we will not be caled in servis   I took diner in the city yesterday with a friend is is the first time I have cit to a table or eat of earthan dishes cince Epps died   I was then nursing him at the hospital   I hardly new how to behave   I hear that all sorts of storyes gets back that is not true   Epps is the only man we have lost our second lieutanant is a man from Binghamton   he has not been hear yet and the last we heard of him he was very sick in Elmira and was not expected to live   we have been marched

out to see two small forts and have a chance to go 1 mile around camp 20 minuts to a tim whenever we are not in drill but the oficers are groing more strict every day   but I must close and may God bless you an the children and keep and protect us all till we meet again and now good by from your loving husband
W A Robinson

Direct Washington D C
    89 Regiment
    NYV Co I or care
    Cat England
our leter has been chanded from H to I

Jan 10th 1862   This short letter is headed: On board the ship Arican. It is written on blue, lined paper which is embossed in the upper left corner "Croton."

Daer wife   wrote from Anapalas and sent you $5,00   I have express $15,00 more to Aaron Hunt $5,00 is four you   send as soon as you can for it   W Halsted sent some to home and wished me to menshion it   I am well and heathy and takin comfort   I sent Penfield $5,00 to him   when you write let me know how much has got around   I have made $20,00 cince I got my pay which was monday and to day is Friday   had I not ben to careful I could have maid $40,00 more just as easy   keep this to your self   it is getting dark   I shall write agane the first opertunity and now good by

William A Robinson

Jan 27th 61 (this letter was actually written in 1862) The letter is headed: On board ship Afracan Hatras inlet.

Dear Mary   I agane adress you   it is the first chance cince I last wrote   I am well and harty and hope this will find you the same   it is 3 week to day cince we shipped and 3 days after tomorrow cince I tuched land but expect to today   I have but litle time to write but can send agane in a week   I send you $5,00 in this   if you have enough pay M Andrews   you can send it to Hunt

I will send you $5,00 more next week   I have sent 15,00 to hunt 5,00 was for you   I sent 5,00 to you and 5,00 to J Penfield   But I must close   good by and God bless you and the children
W A Robinson

Feb 6th 1862 This letter is on heavy stationary paper embossed in the upper left corner. It is headed: Hatrass Inlet

Dear Mary   I now take my pen in hand to adress you   I recived your of Jan 4 day befor yesterday   I am looking for another the next mail and hope I shall not be disipointed   I am well and harty and hope this will find you the same   I have had quite a time   left Washington the 6th Jan arived at Anapolas at night snoozed in the cars till morning stood around (in the most snow I have seen all winter which was about an inch) all day and went aboard the ship Aracan had the

soft side of a plank to sleep on for four weeks lacking 2 days and just room enough to lay on at that   we left Fortress Munroe the Sunday after shiping and anchored off cape Hatrass the next day right in the osion and lay there towe weeks then pased in to pamlico sound and lay there till we landed   we are now tented on a sandy beech about half way betwen the cape and Hatrass inlit   we are in a beautiful place in a grove of live oak and holly   the are boath evergrean   it is swampy around us and would be unhealthe in the

sumar but the news has arived hear to day that Manasas is taken   if that is so the war will close and we will be home by the first of may if things keeps on in this way I shall not ask for a furlough at presant for I do not wish to come home till I come for good   you must not think I did not take comfort on board   the Arircan   for I like it first raight   the first weeke was as pleasant a weeke as I have pased cince I left home   but I begun to want to get ashore before we landed   Halsted is in the tent with me and

him and me are brothers   we eat sleep and stay to gather   I want you to wright as soon as you get this and tell m how much money has got there   I have heard from that I sent by express   I have sent $100 to you by male and $5,00 to penfild   I send $200 in this and will send more soon   adress

Co I   89 NYV
Burnside expidition
Hatrass Inlet

good by and God bless and protect you
William A Robinson

Feb 21st 1861   This letter is on a single bifolded piece of paper which [8] is embossed in the upper left corner. It is headed: Hatras Inlet

Dear Mary
                Agane I take my pen in hand to address you   I am well and harty only weying 160 lb   am well suited with the sirvis but affal homesick   the last leter I had from home was 2 weeks day after to morow that was dated Jan 4th I want to hear from you   bad we are ordered to move to Roanoack Island and expect to start soon probably to guard the 3000 priseners that was taken there last week   it is about 40 miles from

Inlet   I think ther is very litle danger of our geting in a fight as we seem to be kept in the rear of the army as reserve   there is considerable sickness in the rigiment and some in our Co but thank God I am well and every prospect of being so   I can see how to apresiate good health hear   I never was so healthy a winter before in my life   the resion I do not write is acount of being in tents and badly crowded when ever ther is time to write and there is no use in writing only when the mail is going out

which is once in about 10 days   I want to know how much of the money has arived that I have sent and how much you will want next

---

[8] This letter is actually dated incorrectly, as it was written in 1862.

pay day which will bee by the 10th of March   write the very day you get this and direct to Co I 89 Rig NYSV Roanico Island NC   I send you one dolar in this   when I get my next pay I shall send by express to A Hunt   I think it will be there by the 20th of March so you can begin to look for it then whither you hear from me or not   I shall send

$20,00 any way and more if you want it   I think that is all I have to write at presant so now good by for the presant and may God protect you and the children and give us a spedy meeting
   From your loving husband
               William A Robinson

March 2nd 1861[9] This letter does not have a heading.

Dear Mary
         I agane take this opertunity of sending you a line   I am just giting over one of my bilious turns   have been unwell for 3 days but the good news I have herd makes me fee as well as ever   I am quite shure that the war is over   you will hear all the news long before this will reach you   we are on Roanoco Island in a very prety plase   level as a house flore and suround by pines   I like the sirvis well but O home

how I long to be there   I have heard nothing from you since the 4th of Jan   that is a long time to wait but I am afraid my leters does not reach you   I have sent 13,00 in leters to you   we will git our pay in les than 5 days   I shall send by express the first opertunity but fear it will take some time so do the best you can   I think the first of may will see me home if my life is spared and I fel shure the last batle has been fought and I have

not shot a gun yet   I have you and the children in the care of Almighty God knowing that he is more able to take care of you than I   it will be some time before I shall have a chance to send another leter as the mail dose not run regular here   we expect to stay here about 2 weeks and then moove some where but the soldier never knowes where till he gets there   and now good by and my God give us a speady meeting
               W A Robinson

---

[9] This letter is actually dated incorrectly, as it was written in 1862.

March 13 th 1862 The heading is: Camp Dickinson Roanoke Island

Dear Mary   agane I take my pen in hand to adress you   I am well and hop this will find you the same   we have not got our pay yet but expect it every day   when I get it I shall send it the first opertunity I have by express   I should send money in every leter I wrote if I knew that they went safe but I do not hear anything from you so I cannot tell whither you do from me or not   I I know it is not your falt that I get no leters but I have no way of knowing the reason if

you have not recived any news from me cince I have from you   I think you must be woryed enough about me and   God aloan knows the feelings I have had   the last leter I recived was dated the 4 of January   that is a long time to wait but if I could only know the reason   Halsted recived a leter the last male but it said nothing about you   I try to keep up my spirits but many is the tear that I shed when aloan and while the rest in the tent are sleeping   .could I have known the anguish of the sole it would cost me I never could have

left home but my trust is in the all wise God knowing that he orders all things for our eternal wellfare and though we cannot see and know - as we pass along still we have his word and that is enough to convince us that he leads us in a way that is for our good   we have lost another boy cince we arived on this island   it is the third in the Co   it was Bur Bronson of Franklin   he was buried in marshall stile at sun down   the musick ahed then the corps born by 8 men folowed by 8 men 4 abrest and armed   the rest of the Co

2 abrest folowed then the Chaplain Captain and Liutenant   there was singing and prayer at the grave then the 8 men fired there guns over the grave   it was the most solemn funeral I ever atended and O the feelings I had at the grave thinking of his parents and frinds and of you   how you would fel if I was layed there instead of him but God will order for the best and he had some wise purpos in taking this one from our number and leaving the rest   we have 3 sick on the other Island but hear that they are giting beter   there is one sick hear that I fear will not live

I want to know whether you can stay this summer where you are as soon as posable and how you get along for money and if Charly talks or Danny walks yet and all about home   I have litle hopes of geting home till some time in may   I think the war will close by that time if it should turn and not be likely to close I shall try to get a furlough if we stay where we ar it will not be hard to get one any time or if we moove farther north but if we should go south it would not be so easy

I gues I have told you all I can at presant so now good by and may god bless and protect you and the Children   I leave you in his care knowing that he can do beter by you than I can and he has pomised to protect such as put their trust in him

Direct
    Co I 89 Regiment NYSV
    Ronoake Island VA
    From your afectinate
    Husband
        W A Robinson

March 15th 1862   This letter is headed: Camp Dickinson.

Dear Mary   I
take my pen in hand to inform you that I recived two leters from you yesterday and they were like oil on the trouble waters   I can now sit down contented between drills   I got a leter from Sarah[10]   she is at Deposit was well and said she had heard from the other girls a short time before and they wer wel   Sarah was very much troubled about me   said she did not know but she was writing to the dead   I have answered it and wrote to Mary[11] so they will know that

I am in the land of the living yet   I should have got you first leter sooner but the male layed at Hattrass Inlet about a week   they are trying to get a daily mail to Hattrass   if they do we can hear from each other oftener than we have for the last 3 months   you wanted to know how I got along in making money   I can tell you in the next leter that I write as the pay master is here and we will get our pay monday   then I can setle up and see how I stand   I had some bad luck as well as good

I lost $10,00 in one speculation but it was what none could have forseen   I get the large sun of $13,00 per month   the only benefit I

---

[10] Sarah Robinson, sister of William
[11] Mary (Robinson) Slusser, sister of William

get for my ofice is in guard duty as privates stand guard once in from 4 to 8 days while I come on in from 16 to 24 days and then do not have to be out in the weather   I was weighed agane the other day becked down 160 lb easy and the boys say that I look beter than they ever saw me before   I can chow down about 2 rashions of Pilot bread easy and if a little hungry could take 3

I do not pay the postage on my leters as I can get no stamps and there is no post ofice hear so they will not take money and when I send money it will come mor safe   I think you had beter stay where you are as long as Jane is wiling and I want you to get the numars (?) wood if you can   I will keep writing and send money in every leter now I know you get it till I send $25,00 any way   I paid the Captain and Cormack $10,00 each that I had sent you and used for other uses that way $20,00 and $15,00 by express and $13,00 to you in leters and $5,00 til the stamps that is

20,00
15 00
13 00
<u>5 00</u>
total $53,00

I drew $45,00 then I have bought a good myany litle things to eat such as buter at 60 cts per pound and aples 5 cts apeace and I shall have some money when I get setled up so you can judge that I have maid somthing and I think my chance is good to make a few dolar this pay day but you must keep this to your self   then if I shoul hapen to loose instid of mak the folks cannot laff at you

J O Donell[12] go mad and threw up his ofice whill we wer on hatrass and Jacobs[13] is in his plase   otherways the ofisces remain the same as before   J O D got a leter from Jenny McDananil   she says that Dan is very poor and John has a mortgage on all that he has but I do not know any more by that   but it is time to close this leter as I shall send another by the same male and will try to get my mind fried   so now good by and God bless and protect you and the children
William A. Robinson

March 31st 1862   This letter is headed: Camp Dickinson, Roanoak Island

---

[12] Jeremiah O'Donnell, then first sergeant of Co. I
[13] Ira D. Jacobs being promoted from corporal to sergeant

Dear Mary

I agane take my pen in hand to adress you   I recived your last leter in good time and was glad to hear from you   it seams you had not got my last which had $5,00 and a 10 ct Rebble bill in   we have not got our pay yet and I think it doubtfull if we get it till the first of may but we may   if we do I shall send home enough to pay your debts right away   when I wrote the last I expected our pay the next day and should have wrote agane

that day   my health is as good as ever yet and I was glad to hear that you was so well   I begin to think that we shall not get off by the first of may but the war can not last very long   we got new coat saturday they are nice frock coats and it makes us look a great deal beter   but I do not know what to do with mine as my state coat is good yet for three months   but I must war the coat on dress parade and revues we had a revue to day   there was presant the NY 9   New Hamphier 6th and the bludy 89th   we had to march 3 miles in heavy

marching order and it made me think of the hero that luging knapsack box and gun was harder work than farming   we started at 9 and got back at 12 and did nothing more to day but dress parade which ocopyed about a ½ our   the day we got on this Island I saw Ed Lovgran a cosin of Charly   cince that I saw Jim Radigin that was so noisy at camp meeting when we was on the farm   he can sware as fast as any soldier   now you must tell Olive that Halsted is doing a good buisness   he is working at his traid and I think he will get 40 cts extry this day

and tell her that he is geting to be a first raight cook   I have eat a good many pancaks of his manofacture and they ant to be sneased at   our drill is very light hear   only 4 ½ hours per day but it is so divided that with kooking and roal call that we have but litle time to write and when we do the conveniances is so bad that I dread giting at it so you must excuse my not writing oftener   Henry England write to Oppy (?) that you was in his store the 11th so you see you cannot gad about without my hering of it if I am in North Caronina

I take this opertunity to cosion you aganst giting trusted at Englands store as I have heard of very scaly tricks practised on soldiers wives cince we left there by those that I can not doubt their word and if the tribe at home is like the Captain I would not like to give them much of a chance for I would not trust him as far as I could throw a meating house for a man that will sign papers in the army that is not corect is not a safe man to trust any whare but keep this still and distroy this

sheet as I do not want to be the means of leting the cat out of the bagg she will get out soon enought without bisides he yet has power over me though he is more afraid of me than I am of him and when you have money to spend you can do as well some where els I would also cousioun you about Henry England as I know him to be an oily tinged lisensious vilin you may think that this is as neadless or that I am geting jilious but neather is the case but he is so well known that foundation for

starting a story might hapen before you was aware of it so you must not take a timly word from me amis I am giving you a good long leter this time as I am citing up Dan Lea who is quite sick and thretened hard with a feaver I shall go to bed at 2 oclock ther is 16 men snoring aroun me now they keeps good time and make good music for me to write by you might think I could write any night when I could not sleep but we are not aloud a light in the tent after 9 oclock except in case of sickness

so it is an ill wind that nobody good you wanted to know how I got along on board the Acracan it was the pleasantest journy I ever had but amost to much of it at the last end the storm that you heard of was not very bad though for those that was sea sick I supose it seamed afull I was not sick a bit we had plenty of water the most of the time but it was not very good I can not say I suffred for drink for when my canteen ran out I could always get a drink in the forecastle as the salors and yankee was on good tirms

you had beter get what wood you can or enough to last till after haying as you will be bothered to get it after spring work comences and you shall have the money to pay for it by the 10 of may any way as I can get it of Cormack if I do not get pay in seson if you must have more money I can get it for you any time I send you $5,00 in this it is all I have now but when there is any money or any good thing in the Company yankee can have his share but I gues I have wrote about as much as you will want

to read at onece so now good night and may the blessings of heavin rest upon you and the children and may we all live so that if it be gods

will that we do not meat on earth we may meat in heaven   may God be with you keep and protect you and grant us a speedy meeting is the prayer of your loving husband
William A Robinson

Undated. This letter is placed by content as early April 1862. The heading is: Va Delaware st, Camp Dickinson, Roanoak Island.

Dear Mary

I imbrace this opertunity ary writing a line to you   ther will come a leter by mail at the same time   the mail has come to night   I expect to hear from you again   I have sent $10,00 in two leter that I have not heard from yet   write after the litle box that has the testament in   the shells belongs to Halsted   he is in the Hospital I do not know what he wants done with them   I will find out in a

fiew days and write   he is some sick but not very bad   the doctor told me that he was geting beter and would be well in a few days so as to get around   I shall get a pas to see him in a day or to and write agane   I have but a minute to write to night   I do not know as you can read this   Good by and may God bless you and the children Yours till Death do us part
W A Robinson

PS   the penny that you find in the box I gave 25 cts for   take good care of it   I am as well as ever
W A Robinson

Apr 8 th 1861[14]   This letter is headed: No 1 Delaware st, Camp Dickinson, Roanoke Island

Dear Mary

As I have been lucky enough to escape drill to day I thought to improve the opertunity of writing a fiew lines to let you know that I am well and hearty and hope this will find you the same I do not know as I have any news to write that would interest you except we have not got our pay yet and not much hopes of geting it very soon though we are promised it by our oficers but that is geting an old story   I am contented and hapy as can be expected though there is not an hour when I am awake when I do

---

[14] This letter is actually dated incorrectly, as it was written in 1862

think of the loved ones at home and wonder when the time will be when we shall again be united though the time seemes to fly on Eagles wings yet it seams a long time cince we parted and it lookes like a long time to wait for this unholy war to close before I shall see you again but I shall wait with paicience for the presant prospects is that the hard fiting is about closed but it will take time to setle up and discharge the vast amount of troops now on hand   we heard that York Town was taken with 168 canon   the rebls cannot fight much longer if they keep loosing thier arms in the way

they have for a time back   Bob Zeh is well and talks as much as ever he is in the tent with me   we have got a new tent to day so we will not be so thick after this   the weather is warm hear but not so warm as I expets   the night is coole and an overcoat comes in play in the evening some times   we have got new coats as I told you in my last and also a blouse for such as wanted them   I sold my state coat for 75 cts and took one   the coat was worth more than that but it was to warm to drill in   tell Hanah[15] that if she does not like to see men dresed in blue she would not

like to see our regimint in their fatigue dress as it is a dark blue blouse just the cut of my old blue sock and light blue pants that now they are dirty looks like my old overalls   so you know that I am satisfied with my working dress   Dan Lee is worse then he was when I wrote last and has gone to the hospital now but I have not had a night sleep since I wrote last for though I got rid of drill by nursing him I could not get rid of guard duty and my time come and I had to go but I get a resting day to day and shall try to improve it to good advantage

Hasted has been unwell for some dayes back   he took a heavy cold and had a bad headache   the doctor has given him some medicin he thinks he is getting beter now but does not feel like writing so you had beter hand this to Aunt Lib and then the folks will not wonder that he does not write   he sayes he has wrote two leters cince he has recived an answer   we have not had any mail in some dayes   he nor I had any news in about 15 dayes   the last leter I had was dated the 16 of March   there is a mail at head quarters now   it will be distributed to day and we are boath ancious as we boath expect leters from

---

[15] Hannah Sackrider, Mary's sister

home   Halsted has been at work on a dock here and we think he will get extry pay for it   he sends his repects to all and hopes this will find all well   the mail has just come and no leter for Halsted but two fo me   one from you and one from M E & W Sluser[16]   they are well and going on a farm   will keep 9 cows and take possesian the 1st of april   they say the snow has been very deep there this winter and I hear that it has been so in Delhi too   I have not seen even an inch of snow at a time this winter and not even a dosen frosts cince I left Washington   so you see I have not suffred much from

the cold   you did not say there was any money in the last leter you got   I have sent to leters with $5,00 apeace in and a rebel 10 cts bill I want you to keep that safe if you get it and be carful and let me know how much money you get   this is the 4th leter I have recived from you so I have heard from all the money but the last two that I wrote   I have no money now to send but if you get hard up I can get Cormack to write home and you can have just as much as you want but if you can get along with out I had rather you would fo I have asked a good many favors of him already

he is a man where ever he is and one that knowes that this world was maid for more than one man and that man himself   but it is time I closed so now good by and God bless you and the children   tell Charly he must not let Dannie beat him in talking

From you Loving husband
                    William A Robinson

Apr 21st 1862. This letter is headed: Roanoke Island

Dear Mary
            I take this opertunity of writing   a line to you I am well but about tired out   we have had one of the greatest forsed marches that ever was   we left camp on Friday   morning on stamer and landed at 12 oclock at night and by being misguided marched 34 miles when it should have been 15 and Saturday was hot as a July day hundreds give out by the way   about 3 oclock we come up with the enemy and

---

[16] Mary E. (Robinson) and Wesley Slusser, Wm.'s sister and brother-in-law

whiped them "right smart I recon"   we was about 2 houres about it we lay on the field till about 9 oclock when we got news that they wer reinforced   we wer ordered up and started for out boats   it rained about the time we got through the batle and maid the roads ancle deep in mud and we got to our boats just after day light in the morning and just got aboard when the rebles come up   we got back and comenced going ashore about 12 oclock Sunday night   but I will give you the

whole particulars as soon as I get rested   ther was none of our company hurt and nowe comes bad news for others   the first things I herd when I got on shore was the death of W Halsted   he died at 8 oclock on Sunday morning and this morning Cormack and me went to the hospital and did the last (?) ofice for him   he will be buried tomorow morning   I have his last pay and the charg of his efects   I want his friends to send me word how I shall send his money   he will draw another pay the 10 of the next month   I shall

take charge of that also   show this leter to his friends   I will write to them as soon as I can and tell them all about him   I sent $30,00 to Hunt by express   draw what you want and have the rest with him   Good by and God bless and protect you
                    William A Robinson

send me some stamps to pay postage with as I can not get them hear
  I recived yours of the 13th this morning
                    William

Apr 22nd 1862. The heading is: Roanoke Island

Dear Mary   I now take pen in hand to give you a description of the batle in camden co N C   we wer orderd to be ready to start at sun down on monday nigh to start on an expidition and we did not know where and we wer kept in rediness till thursday and began to think it was given up till friday morning   we wer orderd to be ready at a half hours notis   at between 9 and 10 the order came and at ten we wer in line and started about 12 from he dock   we left the boat about 12 at night and landed in a cornfield of about 10 achers   it was moon light and quite warm   about 2 oclock we took up the line of march suposing we would mee the enemy by 8 in the morning   the 9 NY took the lead the 89 next and the 6 NH folowed leaving the 51 penn and 21 Mass to cover our retreat   all to gether maid about 3000 men

at sunrise we heard hevy guns on our left and began to think the batl had opened with our gun boats that had gon up the river   the resirvis herd the fire and thought we wer atacked and started after us   they got ashore and started about 10 oclock   they took the right road and we the rong and at 12 oclock they found them self ahed of our division and wated 2 hours for us to come up   we had 2 howitserzs with us and merins to work them   they then took the lead of the other division and started on   about 3 we heard the enemy guns ahed and we wer huried on   we had marched about 34 miles and at least on third of our men had give out   the rest huried on and soon saw the smoke   the 51 and 21 marched on the left and the 9, 89 and 6 the right   the marins planted three canon in the center and went in to them hansom   as we went up to canon balls pased over the heads of Co I 89 rather to close to be agreeable and there was some handsome dodgin done

but nobody hurt   we then went in a piece of woods and wated for the merines to silence their batery   in about 20 minets the order came to move on and then came the tug of war   as soon as we left the wood a charge was orderd   the 9 led on with a yell and the 89 was close behind and not a man srunk   the 9 was repulsed and the 89 was disorderd and our Colonel orderd them to form under the cover of a point of wood   we wer formed in 5 minutes time and orderd to charde   a fiew of the 9 went in within us and with a yel and a bound we started with bayonets fixed and made for the enemy in good earnest   as we comenced the charge the 21 and 51 pored in a voly and the enemy got up and skadadled right hansom   we then formed in the field to take a rest   after 28 hours excushion and to make the fun compleet there came up a shower that wet us "quite smart I recon"   but tired and worn out we laid down in the field we had nobly won and wer soon sound asleep but at 9 at night we got news that the

enemy had been reinforsed to 10,000 men to atack us in the morning I have my doubts about this but if they had we would have given them a lusty hunt as our straglers had all come up and we had the earth works that we had drove about 2100 fresh men from with about 1800 that could hardly get one foot before the other   but however a silent retreat was orderd and we started   the roads was clay and the rain had maid them shoe deep in mud and a we had a drisiling rain at times but we took the right road back and daylight we got back to our boats having marched 14 miles in the mud and by the time we got aboded the straglars had nearly all com up   we had detroyed a bridge about 2 miles back but some sayes that the rebles came in right just as we started and about 12 oclock on Sunday night we comenced landing at the point about 1 mile from our camp   Got to my tent about 1 oclock Monday morning and it was 8 before the men all got hom and the most foot sore and ragd lot of men I ever saw

We have just heard that the enemy met a reinforcement about 2 miles from the enemy and became panick stricken and retreated in hast to sufolk   but wer within 20 miles of norfolk where 150 000 men lay so it was time to get up and dust   our los was between 15 and 20 killed and 60 or 70 wounded   thers was over 40 that we know of killed and we do not know how many wounded as they had (?) on the field and caried them off as fast as they fell   there was none killed in the 89 and only about 10 or 12 wounded   one is mortal I think in Co A   this I supose the worst of all   Jery Odonell got so drunk that he could not stand just afer we landed on the main land and we had to leave him   he was picked up and got on board the boat in the morning   he is now under arest and will have to stand a cort marshal

I wrote a leter to you last night   it started this morning Tuesday   I have got about over the march   we buried Halsted to day   I will write to John the description of the funeral   ask him to see the leter it will come in the same mail with this   I have not got setled up with all the boys yet so I cannot tell what I have maid but I have sent home $22,00 more than I have due and have $30,00 left so I have maid $50,00 any way and if I do not loose any that is owing me I shall have $10,00 more and am making money every day cince pay day   I can mak $10,00 per month in or on average when there is money in camp the pay master said we would get our next pay by the 10 of may ceritain   when we got our nex pay there will bee a chance to send agane by express and I want Halsteds friends to give direction how they want his mony sent and I will send it then   I shall send more for you then and what you do not want Hunt can keep   it is safe there as any place it can bee   but say nothing to any one that you have any more than you

want then you can keep it aganst I do not get pay reglar again   if some knew that you had mony they would knew it for a day or two and when you kneeded it you would not have it   if you see Hunt before I write to him tell him to deep dark two   I shall write to him as soon as I get tim   I sent some things to Hunt to send to you and a leter with them   let me know when you get them   I recived a leter from you last Sunday week and another yesterday   it seems you had not got but one leter with money latly   I have sent two   one had a secesh 10 ct bill in   let me know if you get both   I told you yesterday that I had sent 30,00 to Hunt   no more at presant   good by and God watch and protect you and the children   I committed yu to his care when the boolits was flying round my head like hail and had full confidence in his power and will and can say that I did not fear to face death   From you loving husband

William A Robinson

On the reverse side is added:

I had a quart of milk for my diner to day   the first I have had cince I left Washington   it only cost 15 cts   may be you dont like it   I dont know

---

May 1st 1862 This letter is headed: Roanoke Island

Dear Mary
            I now take pen in hand to adress you   I am well and healthy and hope this will find you the same   I have not heard from you in some time out cince I wrote last but we have not had a male till to day and then not half a one but expect one to morow or next day   Send me some stamps about 10 as I can not get any heare   I have not news and but litle time so good by and God bless you and the children from your loving husband
        W A Robinson

May 9th 1862 This letter has no heading. After the letter's closing, there was another page written and enclosed with this letter.

            Dear Mary
                        I write to inform you that I am well   I rcived yous of the 20th about the 3 of May   you leters is about 10 dayes coming when the mail comes regular but some times we do not get amail in 2 weeks   then they are longer   I got a leter from Mary and Fannie dated the same day   they wer well   Mary had mooved in a hous by herself and they are going to farming on there own (?)

26

we expect a mail to morow and I hope that I shall hear from Halsteds friends I have got all his maters straightend hear I have but litle to write to day I am enjoying myself as well as I could any whare away from home we have a slack roap to do tricks on and I play chess with Charls Febig and rounce with Lieu Puffer

of Co F and spend the balance of my time speculating when I am not on duty which is but a small part of my time I am geting tough fat and lazy it will com hard to go to work when I get home as I am geting so I dred an hourese drill worse than I used to a dayes work and I hate to write becaus I cant bare to get up to get the ink and paper The weather is coole here the most of the time but we have a warm day once in a while that would do creadit to July or August
I have no more to write at present so good by and may God protect you and the children and wache over you and grant us a speedy meeting which is my prayer in the name of Christ our Lord
    William A Robinson

I must tell you that Cormack thinks of you some times for once on drill my bayonet droped off and he sayed that I must fasten it on beter or some one mite be a widow and just as we was going on the batle ground at Camden he thought my wife would go crazy if she knew what dirty hands I had The day was hot and dusty and they did look affal but I thought you would have thought but litle of that if you had known where I was at the time
    W A Robinson

May 18th 1862. This letter is headed: Roanoke Island, and is on legal size paper with some writing in the margin, stating, " I send you som fish scales in this".

Dear Mary
    I agane take my pen in hand to adress you I am well and hearty and hope this will find you injoyin the same blessing there is some talk of our leaving this Island soon but I hope that when we leave hear it will be to start for the North the news is so imperfect by that I cannot tell what to think about the length of the war but if the stories is true we will be home by the 4 of July if not sooner I am satisfied that some rigiments will be mustered out soo but can not tell whether it will be from the Burnside expidition or not but I hear that we have the promis of being the first discharged if the southerners ar determined to fight to the last it will take all summer to

annihilate them but I think that they maid up there minds to give up Lieutenant Puffer of Co F has resigned and is going home   I shall embrace the opertunity of sending some

money.   I shall send $50,00 but shall lend $20,00 to Case[17] as we have not got our pay yet and his wife has been very sick and she neads money and it is safe as his pay that is due is good for it   this makes $72,00 that I have sent more that I have hear and I have enough left to setle up all that I owe hear and if I do not loose any I shall have some left   so you see I am doing beter than I could at home and this will pay for the seperation   keep up good courage and do the best you can and trust in God that we may meet agane and be enough beter off to make up for the anxiety of the past   I have not heard from you cince the 20th of April   we had a mail the 16 but no leter for me   we had one the 10   I got a leter from Dan and Hanah[18] and one from the old maid[19]   she takes on offal about me but I think she will live it through   no more at present   Good by and God bless and protect you and the children
From your Loving husband
        William A Robinson
I se the papers Gives great acounts of the batle of camden
W A R

May 22, 1862   This letter is headed: Camp Dickinson   Roanoke Island.

Dear Mary
        I agane write a fiew lines to you   I got the things and leter you sent by Jacobs to day and the next leter you sent also   I was glad to hear from you   I can tell you as the last I had heard from you was dated Apr 20th I was glad to see the stamps to as I am ashamed to write to any but relations   the money I spoke of in my last did not goo till to day   we got our pay to day   I have sent $60,00 for you leave it to Hunts till I come or you want it   I have $30,00 left   I send $20,00 fo Halsteds money and $20,00 for Case so I got pay what I lent him before it started   I shall write to Hunt to Day   I am so busey seteling up that I can not write   I am well but this is an old

---

[17] David Case, Pvt. Co. I
[18] This is probably Daniel and Hannah (Sackrider) Bowker, Mary's brother-in-law and sister
[19] Sarah Robinson, at the time an unmarried 35 year old

story   I do not know but you get tiered of hearing it   in hast From you ever loving Husband
                         W A Robinson

On the reverse of this is penned:

I have sent another box to Hunt   there is a Rebble Coat   look in the pockets a pare of pants   the books are Halsteds   giv them to Mrs. Whitney   ther is a specemin of our daily bread
                         W A Robinson

May 29th 1862   This letter is on special commemorative paper with a soldier and flag logo in three colors, and has a printed verse on the stationary. It is headed: Roanoke Island.

Dear Mary
         I take my pen in hand to adress you   the mail came yesterday and no leter for me which droped my under jaw som   I am well at presant but have had a bad cold and head ache   ther is litle arond here since I wrote last so I have but litle to write   I sent $25,00 more mone cince I wrote before making $85,00 in all   I have 20, left so I have made a cool hundred above wages but keep dark for we do not know what may

turn up   leave it where it is and get Hunt to give you a note without Interest for $50,00 payable the first of Nov and one on demand for the rest   then it will be safe if anything shall hapen to him   get the notes in you name
         I got tired of sirving as corporal a while ago so I resigned which raise the ire of Colonel Fairchild and was ordered under arest but could not put an oficer in the guard house for slight ofences so all he could do was order me to kee my tent which I did   when he was in sight and went all over

camp when he was out of sight   I did not have to stand roal call or drill   this lasted 2 weeks and 3 dayes   the boys said they would all like to get under arest too as the wether was very warm but the Col finding I was like to hold out finly let me have my own way and ordered me on duty monday last   So you can let the children play with the neighbours now as their father is not Corporal any longer my pay is the same as before $13,00 per month   David Dixon takes my place   I have not heard anything of the old maid in some time so I gues she has got over

wory about me and by the way I will write to the miror[20] my self when I want my leters published as the pulick will make no alowance fo the confusion of the tent when writing and a hundred other surcanstances for they dont know it any more than H Ricards cows knew that the wall went a foot under ground　but the paper is abot filed up so I will bid you a good by and God bless and protect you till I return　from you ever loving husband
W A Robinson
Inclosed is a note telling Hunt ho to give notes to you
WAR

June 2nd 1862　This letter is on commemorative paper again with the verse and graphic in three colors. It is headed: Roanoke Island.

Dear Mary　the mail came to day unexpected and brought news from you up to the 23　this is the quickest time ever maid cinc I arived hear　you must keep up your courage remembering God is hear and death is every whare and none is safe any where　I am well and hearty yet　the weather is warm but I saw as hot wether in June before and had to work all day harder than now while now I work 4 hours　I think I can stand the heat as well as any one

so I do not fel alarmed　I got a leter from the old maid to day　she takes on afal　it was enclosed in a note to Capt England as she thought I might be dead　the health of the Rigiment is improving it is as good as could be expeted　our camp is kept clean and our tents is comfortable so I aprehend no danger from camp deseases Sarah want you to write　do write and console her　she is at Deposit　I shall write to her this male and tell her where to direct to you　if she feels as bad as she writes she will wory her life out soon and I supose I shall

be answerable for her death　I can read all you writes easy and would like to know if you can do the same　I want you to write often if it is but a lines for when the male comes and I do not get a leter I feel sour all day

I like the servis well as I can make more money hear than any where else and the thoughts of making you comfortable compensates me for

---

[20] Bloomville Mirror, the local newspaper near Mary's home

all the hard ship and danger that I have to undergo   but money will not pay me for the seperation and I have some times think how foolish I was to leave home and I hope that if I get safe back

I will know how to prisz home and stay where I can get home when I wish   if the war is like to last long I shall com home if money will fech me and I think money and sharp practise will for if the Colonel will not let me come I will try Burnside and he is a king hearted man and if asked in a right way I think I could get the privelage   but I see the papers is giting full and I will bid you good by   I leeve you and the children in the care of one that is more able to take care of you than I   From your ever loving husband   till Death do us part
W A Robinson

June 24th 62   This letter is headed: Roanoke

Dear Mary

I agane take my pen in hand to adress you   I recived 2 letters from you   one from Hunt one from NY and one from the old maid day be fore yesterday   it apesed my wrath some   I think it a good joke to scold me about not writing when you wait a good while before you write and then be 11 days writing it   if you have waited 2 or 3 weeks for leters you must have mised some or I do   they have got delayed as I dont think I have

mised over 10 dayes and that not often   You wanted to know what I was seling   tobaca has been what I have delt in most as I have sold about $200,00 worth   I have had cakes crackers chees apels shugar ad other thing food to eat but my store played out about six weeks ago but I can not be idle so I have sent to NY for a lot of books   I expect $20,00 worth to day and I borowed $40,00 yesterdat and started for more   My pay began the 16th of September and thier is 2 months pay due the

1st day of July   The things in the coat pocket was French maches an inck stand a pipe and a patent drinking cup   the paper was put in by mistake   that belongs in camp   the machs I sent in the first box is for stoks to the pipe but you nead not smoke in it and get it all black as it is to show where the 89 was on the 19 April   the pants I thought would make charly a good pair as I shall never want to see a pair of blue pants when I get home   You say that being printed was none of your doings   I would like to know how

Champ got it   I did not care so much about it but thought I wood stop it before did   as I see it is the fashion to print leters from soldiers and if that folks could hear the swaring it caus hear I think they would stop   I did not know that I had sent any leter by male to delhi till you wrote about Mary opening it   it must have bean a mistake but I will try and comply with your request   we had a specimin of a suthern shower last night   the lightening played

about a hower stidy   it was light more than half the time and the thunder did not seas to role atall   we had 7 or 8 as heavy claps as I ever heard   they wer defning   the rain pored down in torants   Case was on gaurd but i have not saw him this morning to know how he liked it   the air was so hevey in the tent durind the shower that I could hardly breath   the swet rold down me as fast as it ever did when

I was moing   I am as well as ever now   a peace of 7 by 9 brodside and a quart of beans and about 6 crackers well dispear down my neck in a very short tim now   but this is all the pape I have got and I stole the whole sheet at that   but I expect a ream to day so I must close so now good by and god bless you and the children and keep us all and grant us a speedy meeting   from your loving husband
                                                W. A. Robinson

July 3d   1862   This letter is headed: Camp Dickinson   Roanoke Island.

Dear Mary
        I agane take my pen in hand to write a line to you   I receved of the 22ond yesterday and was sory you got so scared about me   I was not so sick any time but that I could take care of myself   Dr Page hapened to be on Roanoke makind out the report of sick the day I was the sickest and sargent Jacobs was mad as a march hare because the surgon excused me from drill so I he must have thought

I was not dangerous   I was about 2 weeks unable for duty but have been well and hearty as ever cince   I got over it   I am glad I have had the fever as I will not be likly to have it agane
        We have had two nice rides cince I wrote last   one was up the Albmarl Sound and the other done in the Pamlico   one the last we

started the morning of the first and got back the night of the second last night and
found a leter hear from you

There is some talk of mooving from here in a fiew dayes but I hope we will not go as we are situated beter here than we can be any where els   you need not be surprised if you do not get another leter very quick for if we do moove it will take some time to get in a shape to write   we just heard that Richmond is taken but have not heard the particulars   I hope that thye will take the intire army as that would end the thing
   I dreamed of beng

home last night and Charly talked real good   I do not know as I have any more to write so now good by and God bless and wach over you and the children and grant that we may meat agan on earth if not that we ary meat in Heaven
   From your ever Loving husband
       W A Robinson

July 10th This letter is headed: Camp Dickinson, Roanoke Island

Dear Mary
   Agane I take my pen in hand to adress you   I am well and hearty and hope this will find you the same   we have not mooved yet but I think we shall as the most of the Division has moooved and we have had orders more than a week ago to hold our selves in readyness but direct as usual till I send you word to change the   I have but litle nuse to write   I supose you know that they are fighting at Richmond

yet it is thought here that if that plase is taken with out the Rebels evacuating it will finish the war and every efort is making to trap them there   I think Burnside is mooving in the rear to cut off the last chance of escape and great confidence is plased in his ability to do what he undertakes   our Rigiment is the last in his division so I think we will not see much of the fight if they should moove on to us wheich there is

but litle danger of there doing   but if they do may each man do his duty and conquer af (?) or dy   as for me I had rather leave my body on the field than live a coward   if we moove I shall imbrace the first opertunity of writing to you but there is litle hopes of having a chance for two weeks   I know leave myself you and the children in the hand of him that noeth all things to do as seameth him good and now good by for

the presant and may God in his mercy protect you and the children and wach over you is the prayer of your ever fathful husband
William A Robinson

July 13th This letter is headed: Norfolk

Dear Mary
          Agreeable to my promis in my last which I supose you will not get till you get this I take my pen to adress you.   I am well and hope this will find you the same   we started from Roanoke the 10 at 2 oclock PM and arived here before daylight yesterday   we are incamped close to the city in a very

good place   the 163d 9th and 89th are together in one brigad under Col Hawkens   I think we must be a resirve by the way we ar incamped and by Colone H having the comand as he must be the junier oficer as ther is two Brigadiers in the division and only 3 brigades   the other two has gon on farther towards Richmond before

we got here   wright the verry day you get this and direct to Norfolk Va   I would like to give you a discriptshion of our jurny here but their is so much confusion here that I am Almost crazy so I bid yo a good by and god bless you and the children   from your sorry husband
W A Robinson

July 19th 1862   This is one of the longer letters, and uncharacteristically, the pages are numbered.   The heading is: Norfolk, VA

          Page 1
Dear Mary
          I tak this opertunity of writin a fiew lines to you   we wer ordered to strike tents at 12 oclock on the 10th at Roanoke   at 2 oclock we were underweigh for we knew not where   there was

34

nothing of any acount hapened that day till about 10 or 11 oclock we wer ordered to leave the steamer and go on board a reck of a scooner that had

2   been raised near the camp we had left   we made our selves as comfortable as we could till morning when we found our selves in a narow long sound lined on each side with swamp land that varied from a half to 1 and a half mil in width   we wer towed buy a small steamer   she had two other schooners in tow   about 1 oclock we got through the sound and entered a river with the swamp land

3   about the same as along the sound   just as we entered the river the steam boat cut loose and went back to look after 2 others with 5 schooners in tow leeving us to pass the time as best we could   the water was deep clear to the bank and we got off in the swamp   the mud was not a deep as I expected to find it   we could walk with eas any where we went crost the swamp and some got a fiew buryes

4   when we came back to the schooner one brought a racoon and two brought a mockisin snake apeace   one was about 5 feet long and as big as my ankle   these are more posin than the ratle snake   the stamer got back about three oclock after we had had a good walk and a good bathe and away we started   about this time it began to rain and the deck leeked like a sive and we got glorious wet though we raised our tents on deck and sheltered

5   some   from the river we entered a canall 8 miles long   this was lined along the bank with the nisest buryes you ever saw   in spots the bushes was black with them and sometimes we would run so the bushes would hang over the side and their grating was general and as we was going about 6 miles an hower scraching and pricking was not very rair and one man lost his cap over board   we got through the canall by pasing a lock wich took some time and entered a river

6   about dark and the morning we found selves in Norfolk harber we landed about 10 oclock ad piched our tents about 1 miles from the city though it is 3 miles to get thier by land   the next day after I sent a line to you and the next day got a leter from you and one from Sheldon Hanford   yours was dated the 28   it had been to the Island our sick and 60 able bodied men is left ther and we soon expect to go back but we never know one day where we shall be the next

7   as we ar under orders and never know when they will com and when they don   we never know where we are going till we get there we hear all sorts of stories of when and where we are going and some of the timids will swallow them and write home and bidd all good by and then find out that we are going to stay   there folks thinks they are gon and do not know where to direct and then they get cursed   I have saw this about every time that a yarn has been started   when we left roanoke

8   wrote a week ahed and told that we would start the next day for Richmond   the conseqence is but litle male and a good deal of swaring and we are in Norfolk and likly to stay and as likly to go back as to go to Richmond and a litle more so   the night of the 15th we had an afall thunder shower   I have never heard as many sharp peals of thunder in the length of time it must have everiged one a minute for a half hour   the flash and peal came togather ever time it seamed as if the heavens was shaken in peases

9   and the rain fell by pails full   I was thank full I was not on gaurd that night   the next night was my turn and the 17th I got a pas and went to the city   there is now buisness done there of any concequance and the people look very cross at the US uniform and some of the ladies noses turn up as they pass us in the street   it is a very nice city as far as buildings is concirned but the streets are crooked and in bad repair at presant but I gues I have spun this yarn out long enough   my health is good and I hope this will find you and the children injoying the same blessing   I was glad you got my other leter

10   as soon as you did as I know about how you took on when you thought me sick but I shall tell you the truth as to my health and where we are going as fare as I am cirtain but shall not wory you with camp yarns   now you must not wory at what the rest writes if you hear it as my chance for knowing is as good as any and I can remmemmber when I get fooled a fiew times   no more at presant good by and God bless and protect you is the prayer of your ever Loving husband
            William A Robinson
            Norfolk, Virginiy
all leters will folow us where ever we go

August 17th 62. This letter is interesting in its stationary form. It is written on a special Volunteer's Memento of the Army in Virginia printed in red, white and blue. It includes a song, with verses, printed blanks to fill in unit and to whom written. Written in the blanks is 9th Army Corps, 3d Division, to Mrs. Mary Robinson. In the bottom space for signature is written William A. Robinson, Camp Park, Co. I, Regiment 89th NY. The heading on the letter proper is: Fredericksburgh

Dear Mary

    I recived yours of the 10th to try and hasten to answer it   I am well at present and hope this will find you the same   we have been on detached duty for a few dayes back and returned last night about midnight   there was 1 co of the 9th 1 of the 103rd and Co I under the command of Capt England watching a brdge and a trole bridge it was it was 80 ft high and built of

round timber without a mortis or tenant in the whole bridge   it was about 200 ft long and it looked afall to see the cars going over such a looking structure   I have enough to write to fill 3 sheets but was on guard night before last and came in last night and feel more like sleeping than wrighting so now good by and god bless you and the children is the prayer of your ever loving husband
                W A Robinson

August 23d 1862   This letter is headed: Fredericksburgh, Va

Dear Mary
    I take this opertunity of writing a fiew lines to inform you that I am well and hope this will find you and the children injoying the same blessing   our Co is on detached duty at presant and I hope they will stay a while   we was here once before   we are guarding a rail road bridge about 5 miles from camp   we came here last night and are ordered to stay a week but are liable to be caled back any time or stay a month as we cant tell wehn we get up in the morning where we shall sleep at night   I formed an aquaintance with a couple of sicesh old maides when we wer hear before and am now at there house writing on a table a

Lucsury that I have not had before cince I left home   the way I got acuainted I came here for milk which I get for only 10 cts per qt and was looking at their bees and one of them said she thought one hive had ought to be taken up and wanted me to look at it and see what I thought about it   I found it badly cut with milers and most kiled out and as she had no help to take it up but two stupid nigars and I could as well help as not I thought it had beter be taken that night and it was but while looking in the morning one of the bees from another hive stung me in the eye and it sweled almost shut and the other eye sweled bad   the boys sayed I was geting fat and looked quite handsome

If you could have saw me that night with a sweled fase ane sleeves rouled up and honey to my elboes you would have been scared for fear some of the dauters of Virginia would be captivated and I would secsead   well last night I put a cap on another beehive and the resulet was I got canteen full of fresh butermilk and a super of hot cakes and hunney   I got som sugar this morning and we draw good bakers bread now so you can gues what I had for breakfast   There is great quantyties of peaches that will be ripe soone on cecesh orchards and I rather gues ther will be a good market for them with litle trouble and less pay   the last leter I had from you was dated the 9th and had two stamps in it   I look for another

to day   we have a mail now every day   I got a leter from the old maide this week   se said she expected mother to deposite last saturday so you can expect a visit from her this fall to stay all winter if no longer   I have writin to know if she is out of a home and if se is told her she could have a home with me   I think it would be more pleasant for you if she was there now but I think that this war must wind up this fall as the rebels can not stand the amount of ment that the north is sending up on them and how glad I shall be to meet you and the children agane   it see as if I could come home for one week I could come back contented but I shall never ask a furlough as long as we are plased where we may be caled in batle at any time as I do

not want the name of coward to folow me home   but there is litle danger of our regemint being caled in if there should be a fight near hear as we are detaled as a guard to the town and railroad and they allways have been behind   you wondered how I could stand the heat I do not feel the heat any more than usual as we do not do much when it is hot   we have had a coole stand for a time back and the nights we so coole that we had to rap up in our blankets to keep warm but it

is geting warmer now   but I am geting tired and will bid you a good by and may God bless and protect your and the children and grant us a speedy meeting   From you ever loving husband
William A Robinson

I shall send the leters to Merideth after this a Daniel[21] must be geting through with hayin by this time

August 27th 1862. This letter is headed: Fredericksburgh, Va

Dear Mary
    Again I take my pen in hand to adress a line to you   I am well and hope this will find you the same   our co is still at the bridge and I hope will remain a while   I recived yours that spok of gitin the leter I sent by stilson 3 dayes ago but had just writien so did not hasten to answer it   I want you to lay in as much provision of all kinds as will last till the first of may and pork enough to last till fall I think you had beter get 200 lb   I will write to Martin Smith and get him to save or get it for you   you had beter see Smith or Hunt and get tea sugar and all other

groceryes in one lump to last till May but not get them till they get back from the city   tell them how much you want of each and get your salt at the same time   by doing so they will let you have them as cheap as they can   I have not heard any thing more from mother yet if she should come you must get tea enough   there will be no loss on buying tea as it will get no cheaper for a year to come   if you want any coton goods you had beter get to Delhi and get what you nead all at once and in one plase   that will get no cheeper in a year so do not go in to small as you can do beter with a large bargain and make the store keeper belive you want full as much as you do and the one

will give you the most for $10,00 is the man to get it   we will get pay agan in a short time and I will send you more money as I do not want you to break that note at Hunt & smiths till I get home   I am not making any more than I am spending at presant but may strike another streak of luck   I think that that box of books is at Aqunia crick and will come here as soon as the road is at liberty for the

---

[21] Daniel Sackrider, brother of Mary

express Co to use if it hapens to get here just as we get our pay it will be nise
You want me to send my adress plain Via means by way of D.C. Destrict Colombia so send to Co I 89 Reg NYV Via Washington D.C. Wahsington is not in Virginia as you had it on the last letter

that I got if the leters get started right they will get here if they have the co and Rigment on it directed to Bunga but leave of the Care of Capt England there has tow leters com here with that on that has been to England and it takes quite a while to get around in that direction I have no more to write at presant so now good by for the presant and god bless and protect you and the children is the prayer of you ever loving husband

William A Robinson

W A Robinson
Co I 89 Rigiment NYV
Via Washington D C

Sept 24th 1862 This letter has the heading: Near Sharpsburgh Md

Dear Mary
I imbrace this opertunity of writing a fiew lines to you I am well and hope this will find you the same I sent a line to you from the battle field we have had no fighting since but they had schirmishing on the right that day and the next but the rebles are all gone now I think they did not like Burnsides way of doing buisness we are about 8 miles North West of Harpers fery and expect to go there soon to incamp and rest up we have rested 3 dayes here but since I wrote from Washington we have been eather marching or fighting every day before and we are covered with glory and lice I have enough of both for the presant the 14th we had a twist with the rebls and had about 18 wounded in the regiment but none in our Co the hotest of the fire was on the left of the regiment and it was my luck to be in the rear gaurd and was just turning the left when the fire opened and the bulets

came with a vengence one of the rear gaurd droped dead on the spot and one of Co K wich was right in front of us and 18 wounded all in about one minute the rebels then charged bayonets and our fire opened in there face about 20 droped dead and as many more wounded they broke and flead and Co A folowed and broght in a dozen prisners this was caled the batle of South Mountain the right had been fighting all day and it was about sundown when we wer brought in after they left us they formed and went a litle farther to the right and the 51 NY went into them with a vengance suported by the 51st ohio and piled the rebls up in heaps that lasted till about 9 oclock Mr Alpines sun and Charles Waters is in the 51st they are both well the next day we marched to near Sharpsburgh and was kept in line all day the next day and was Marched on a hill and kept in line all night and got sheled out in the morning one of Co I was wounded John White and about 30 or 40 of the regiment

wounded and none kiled we wer marched from place to place till about 3 oclock when we got under the range of the rebel guns and keched another sheling but this time we went twords the enemy insted of from them Co I was ordered in front of the rigiment as scirmishers and went to the top of a hill and drove the scirmishers of the enemy back we wer then ordered back a litle to let our guns play I had got about 2 rods back when a shell burst on the ground where I had been lying the brigade was then ordered forward and Co I to go in the advance of the 89th a Co of the 9th in front of them and a co of the 103d in front of them we went over the hill and acrosed a ploughed field and up another hill the rebls wer under a stone wall at the top of that hill we had got most to them when they rose up and fires over us and we fired in to them I sliped on a round stone and fell and the rigiment ran over me

I was beat out with hunger and fatgued as I had eat but 6 crackers in 36 houres as we could not get provision on the ground so I lay still about 15 minutes when a brigade of rebels came out of a corn field about 10 rods from me on the left and it would have done you good to see me leave that spot they ordered me to halt but they was not the men I had been in the habet of minding so I kept mooving they sent about 50 mesengers after me but I was to slim for them I got where there was anothe rigiment in a holow and staid there about 15 minuts when the rigment came off the field and I got with them agane but this is all the paper I have so now good by and god bless and protect you and the children and grant that we may meat agan on earth if not may we meet in heave from your ever Loving husband
W A Robinson

Sept 28th 1862. There is no heading.

Dear Mary

  I imbrace this opertunity of writing a fiew line to you I am well and hope this will find you the same I recived yours of the 14th to day and hope to get another soon as ther must be one on the road we have not got our pay yet that should have come the first of this month I supose you hand would have been unstidy when you wrote the 14 if you had known where I was while you was writing there is know prospect of another fight in this part so keep easy the batle that we fought Thursday was caled

the batle of Anteatam you will hear of it our lose was George Gray mising John White Patrick Huse Stephan Wood and Alexis Jones wonded R Zeah S Olmsted Nat Law and D Seymour badly scared Jery O Donel went through this time and done all the fighting every body else eather was cowards or fool hardy inclosed is a leter for Dan and Hanah in close and send as this is all the paper or invelop I can get to day so good by and god bless and protect you and the children from your ever Loving husband

  W A Robinson

Oct 5th 1862 The heading is written: Head For North Antietam

Dear Mary

  I agane take my pen in hand to adress you we have been still cince I wrote you last and are like to for any thing that I can see we had a visit from Old Abe day be fore yesterday we drill a litle and pass the rest of our time hunting Cinse we left our knapsacks at washington and just got them yesterday I puled my shirt of about 10 dayes ago and such a looking shirt it was Oh dear and I dared not lay

it down for fear it would walk of I kiled all I could ketch and then went to the brook and covered it with soap roaled up my pants and went at it I spent the fore noon on it and spred it on the tent to dry and took coole with out a shirt till night when it got dry it looked like a leopard but it was beter than it was before after the cloths cam yesterday I tryed it agane with beter success I have sone angumtam and think I can keep my cloths so they will not walk alone

we are worse of hear for mail than we wer on Roanoke we have not had a male since I rote last and no talk of having any and pay I gues is played out though I heard the pay master was coming week after next ther is 4 months pay due the 1st day of next month I want you to get wood for the winter ingaged as soon as you can where you can depend upon it and let me know how much money you want to pay for all you by this fall as I do not think I shall send any more home than

you need right away but would like to keep 75 dolars at Hunts if you can let me know how much there is the next time you write you had beter look out for what beefe you want soon and as we can not tell how long this war will last you had not beter get more than you think you will eat your self and if I should get home I do not think I shall be home much this winter I had a leter from Wesley

the last male he said Mother was not very well but so as to be around and was contented there and welcom as long as she wished to stay I sent her $2,00 from Washington and if I can get pay shall send her more
I would like to know how Ebb and Meal gets along lately and how Johns folks are I am well and hearty
and hope this will find you the same and till me if the

boys improved in talking and if they grow any but I guess I have wrote enough for this time so now good by and may God bless and protect you and the children now and for ever
From you ever loving husband
        W A Robinson
It would make you heart ache to hear Jery O Donel swear as he has in the next tent cinc I have been writing this he gross worse

every day if he could get what liquor he wanted he would be as bad as ever he was and I think will be any way as soon as he gets out of the army
        W A R

October 8th 1862. This letter is headed: Camp Near Harpers Ferry.

Dear mary

I recived yours of the 4 to night and was glad to hear from you   we moved yesterday and ar incamped and expect to stay for some time here   I got a leter from Frank a fiew dayes ago   I am well and hearty as I ever was in my life and would be glad to know that this would find you the same but have litle hopes of that as long as you keep woring about me

Do you not know that you make you life miserable and indanger you health and in that way wory your self your children and me   I do not wish to chide you but I fel this my duty and have thought of it for some time   and you can not expect to have good health as long as you keep you mind haresed with dark forbodings and the more you give way to them the darker they will be   and it would not take long for you to reach an untimely grave   and does it make the mater any beter   does it

put me in any less danger and do yo think that you r lot is harder than mine that you complain so much to me   or is it harder than many others   there is those who have more children to take care of than you who has husbands in the army that neglects them and have then to take care of themselves and litle one   you have great reason to bless God that you are provided for and can you trust him and murmur at his decreas   you know that if I am struck down in batle that it is well and he has promised to take care of the widow and orphan   but dare you ask him for help in such times as that with the thought in you mind that you always distrusted him whose every promis in in your favor   if you only will excep the turns   and wold it not bare a just punishment to you wer I taken from you if you make an Idol of me and distrust the ever living God   now paus and think and how can you if you Idolize me and stop think wish to put me to the pain you do by constantly complain

and worying to me   now when you have red this think it over and try and turn your mind in another direction   if you mind is ocupyed in some way you will forget for the time being of the danger that surounds me   but the danger is not a tenth part as great as you in your stat of mind would make it out   it is 100 chance to one if there is another batle her and it is al likly for us not to be in it if ther is and if I should go in another batle the same eye waches me that has in the other and the same arm is as powerfull to protect   and now try and chear up and let your houshold duties ocupy your mind and in stid of disponding and not writing keep pen and paper handy and write a line to a time as you get a chance and when it comes time to send it date and finish it   and spend as much time with the neibors as you can and any time you can go to Harpusfield so you can get to Delhi and

take the stage to the head of the river and folks ther will take you over if they cant you can hire a horse and get around to Hobart or to Mothers and take the stag back   the money will be a small object in comparison with you health wich your indangering daily   but I am incroaching on sleeping hourer as it was after roal call we got the male and I expect to be on gaurd tomorow so if I did answer this tonight I should not get a chance for tw dayes as I shall be sleepy and tired the next day   our gaurd duty is not hard at presant as we camp in division and each rigiment help to furnish the gaurd   and now good by for to night and may God wach over you and the children and bless you boath now and forever is the prayer of you ever Loving husband
    William A Robinson

October 16th 1862   This letter is headed: Camp Near Harpers Ferry

Dear Mary
    The male came yesterday but no leter from you but I got one of biter groans from the old maide   every body said that I was dead and she rad in the papers that sombody was dead in Co A in another rigiment and thought it was me and wrote to the Chaplain to know what became of me   I have not saw the Damring cince as he is with the wounded at Antietam but didnt I blow her up to night   gues she will take the hint   I told her if you whined as much as she did I would insist in the C.S. sirvis   It is just a year to day cince we left Delhi and little did I think where I would be today and that this war would still be raging with as litle prospects of closing as it had then but I am bound to take things easy if I can not remidy them   I want to be home as bad as you

Want me to come but I se no way of coming till winter sits in   if the war is like to last but I have strong hopes that the war is fast closing and it may close sooner than we expect   the Sothern Congress admits that they ar starving and that there hopes of sucess is small and they are only fighting to keep there credit up but the fall elections will tell the story as the people will show what they think but I have had a hard dayes work to day and will have to bid you good night and God bless you and the children   From   you ever loving husband

William A Robinson

October 25th 1862   This letter is headed: Near Harpers Ferry

Dear Mary
   I recived yours of the 19th to night and was glad to hear from you and that you was well   I am tough as a buck can eat pork and hard bread in a way that makes Uncle Sam tremble.
   H M Smith is going to let you have a half hog   it will be about 200 lb if it is cheap it is the time to get it   would not care if it was twise that so have barel and salt   Hunt will get you a barel if you want it   if you speck in time Smith sayes he will came over and see you soon   I hope he will and if you till him how you want it he would get the salt and baril and finsh it for you   if you had barel you could send it to Hunt and Smith could get it from them and bring it back there if he wished   S and Hunt could send it up   you can get buck wheat flour at Hunts or corn meal I think and if you want empty flour barels you can get them

get pleanty of every thing as it is as cheep now as any time and things goes farther in large quantitys than small and I may come and help you eat one of these dayes and when I get vituls that is kooked I mean to make up for lost time   You nead not stay where you are only till spring whether I come home ore not   if I come I shall moove any way and if not I can get a place for you that will be more pleasant and I should take the first chance to tell Jane   so as soon as I see any likly hood of the war lasting I will write to Smith and get him to look around for a place for you so you had beter not get wood to last more than the first of April   I fear I have lost the box   it cost $36,00 but I shall try make the express Co pay it if I can   I sent to Hunt for $8,00 and have not heard fro it yet   I orderd it sent to NY   I do not know but that is lost to

as the leters started the sixth   it seams youknew about it or else the money that I lent to Mary Case   that was $5,00   Case has six months pay due him a week from to day and I have four and do not expect it now till the 10 of next month   I want you to inquire when mrs Case pays that and let me know   I recived a leter from you the next day after I wrote my last with some tea in that was worth a gem to me and you may do so every time you write as I have given up drinking the coffee that we have   as for you not drinking tea I think you a foolish   the cost is not great   and I think it will do you good and keep you good natured   I do not want to come home and find you cross enough to bite of ten peny nales   We expect to moove to morow which is our luck   we generaly go Sunday   I hear we are

about 7 miles   it will be a hard days work for us and take about a week to get as comfortable as we are hear but it is all in a life time but I am about our of any thing to say and will stop so good night and God bless and protect you and the children is the prayer of you evr Loving Husband
William A Robinson

October 31st 1862   This letter is headed: Landen Co Va

Dear Mary
    I herd the joyful sound of Co I for male just now and found yours of the 26 and was glad to hear you talk so diferent from usual I am well and hope this will find you the same   the wether has been cold along back but pleasant and is giting warmer   as for pork I have pleanty and would like to send it to you to be cooked

close pleanty but want washing   I have to do Picket duty an then rather often   I see that we was of the same mind about staying with our dear Brother Daniel or Daniel in the lions den if you pleas   We wer musterd for pay to day but may not get it in 2 month to come ther is $52, due to day and I hav not had money enough to sware by in the last month   I hear nothing from that from Hunts yet   would

write to see about it if I had a stamp   we marched Tuesday and agane thursday and may march agan any day as ther is a moove going on but mooving is about all we can do in the 89 as we get but about 230 men on dress pirad adn only 3 captans   1 field oficer and about 8 lieutenants   the oficers have all resigned and gone home and at the rate we are loosing men by discharge and other wise we may

as well all resigne   I would like to any way   so good by for to night and God bless you and the Children   From Your ever loving Husband
          W A Robinson

Nov 9th 1862   This letter is headed: Somewhare in Va

Dear Mary

    I imbrace this chance of sendind you a line   we have had no male since I recived and answered your last   I am not very well at present   my back troubles me but I think it is geting beter   the enemy is retreating and we folowing   we are west from Washington and Manassas is about half now between us and washington   I have muse to write but a bad chance   I write agane the

first opertunity   we will be to some town before long and if I get worse I shall stay   we have no pay yet but I do not care as I could not send it home and do not want it around me   and now good by and God bless you and the children   from you ever Loving husband
                                              W A Robinson

Nov 19th 1862   This letter is headed: Fredericksburgh, Va. On a separate piece of paper that was enclosed is a short directive.

Dear Mary

    I supose you are anxious to hear from me   we got here to day after a long hard campain   we have marched about 100 miles since we left Harpers fery   I got yours that told about the pork the day I wrote last   I hear the male is to aquia creek   we will get it to morow

you did right abou the pork but I think we will stay here and I shall have a chance to write agane soon   I am very tired   I am some beter than I was when I wrote last but my back troubles me   I keep with the boys and that is beter than some of the Co   Good by and God bless you
                                              W A Robinson

send me a dolar and a fiew stamps in your next   send the money in postage convances if you can get it as change is scarce here   we do not expect our pay till the first of Jan
                                              W A Robinson

Dec 2and 1862   This letter is headed: Camp Near Fredericksburgh

Dear Mary

    I agane drop a line to you   I am well and hope this will find you the same   I have had so much to do and it has bee cold hear so I have not writen as a should but I have got the tent fixed with a fire in it now and am comfortable   I have 7 leters to write that had aught to have been writen a week ago   shal write as many as

I can to day   Dan Lee is hear all right   you must have mised one leter that I wrote   I hear that a male was lost and several of our Co has bee scolded on that acount   W got our litle fifty two day before yesterday   I shall send some to the bank in your nam   get it when you want it   it will be behind the leter a week or more   I shall keep more than usual and try to make up what I have lost or loose more   I dot

all you leter regular   I have a good deal that I wanted to wright but forgot what it was   I was down to the old maids yesterday and had a good diner and got a peck of potatus and 5 lb huney   for three of us it will kepp us line for some time   we ar geting beter rations now than when on a march so I think we will live like kings   I can not write any mor to day so good by and God bless you and the Children
    William A Robinson

I got a good Chance to let out my mony and let it go so if you can get of Hunt as you think best sete with him if you like
    William A Robinson

Dec 7th 1862   This letter is headed: Camp Near Fredericksburgh

Dear Mary
    I will indever to write a fiew lines to you   I am as well as usual and hope this will find you the same   we stay in the old plase yet and are like to for any thing that I see   it has been very cold last night but I was warm though many of the boys

suffered with the cold   there is 3 of us in a tent and we fastened the ends up with small sticks and mud and built a fire plase in it and them that laughed at us for working to have cached it last night   we can cook in the tent and make a good hand at it and I shall have to show you how to kook potatoes and make

gravy when I get home   I have all the potatos that I want for when I get out I go to the old maids and get moer   as for meat we get plenty fresh beef   eat beef pork use beans and hard tack coffee that would do justice to a mud hole and I prefur   water and use my sag sugar or crackers   so you see I am not like to starve but as for writing it

is a hard job as is is imposable to get a chance without being jamed in a corner and sit cramped up   I used to think it we wer crowded in the sitty tent but this is as much wors as that was worse than a house we got our pay last sunday   I wrote once and now good by and God bless you and the children   from your ever loving husband
         W A Robinson

Dec. 18th 1862   This letter is headed: Camp Near Fredericksburgh

Dear Mary
         I take this opertunity of writing a fiew lines to inform you that I am well and hole hided yet though I hav been through a heavy battle cince I last wrote   I should hav writen sooner but have had so much to do cince we got back that I had no time   we have no candles so I can not write after dark   to day I am at leasure and will write to the girls when I get this finished

I recived yours with a dolar in it a litle over a week ago and have heard nothing from you since but thought it on acount of being where you could not sent to the ofice   I can not write much to day as it is cold and the days ar short and duty pleanty   I shall send you some money in the course of 3 or 4 weeks   we are in the same camp we was before the batle   I will try and give you an acount of the batle soon but must close now so good by and God bless and protect you and the children and grant that we

may meet soon on earth but if not consistent with his will may we so live as to meet in heave is the prayer of you ever Loving husban
         W A Robinson

De 28th 1862   This letter is headed: Camp Near Fredericksbgh

Dear Mary
         I thought it about time to write a line to you   I am well as comon and taking all the comfort aloud a soldier   I indulge in Idleness the most of the time and go to see the old Mades for a change ever thing here is still and the monotony of camp life is earksome enough   how I would like to have freedom for a short time to see how it would seem

but if I had to go at hard work I think I would get homesick for camp as we do nothing but gaurd duty and dress parade but it keeps us busey to get wood kook and eat and lounge around so I am bothered to get time to write and as ther is nothing doing I have nothing to write the talk here is that the 9 army corps is going in winter quates soon but nobody noes only madam runen we had an adress from old Abe red on parade to night in praise of our conduct

at the batal and the talk is that the first boats of the 89 that crosed the river are to hav a medal from congress I was not one there was 4 from Co I George Hichcock is the only one that you knew I would like the honor and the medal but would rather be excused from a job of the kind they went by detail and if it had been for me to go I should have went but I felt releived when the detail was maid and

me left out but I shall have to close so now good night and may God wach over you and the children and may you put utter confidinc in an an all wise God is the prayer of your ever Loving husband
                    W A Robinson
P S I did not know the trouble you hat in sending to the ofice I should think you was giting lasy
                        WAR

Chapter Two
Letter Transcriptions 1863

Jan 11th 1863 This letter is headed: Camp Near Fredericksburgh. It is written in ink on blue-lined paper.

Dear Mary

I take this opertunity of writing a fiew lines to you   I am well and hope this will find you the same   I have thought a great deal of the way you are situated and about mother   I do not know what she can do if she should be sick long or unable to get round with her leg you must let me know how she gets along as often as you can   I looked for a leter last night but it did not come but I supose you get but litle time to write but try and write once a week if but litle   get Luis[22] to write if you can not so I can know how you get along then for you are in my mind the whole time and I do so hope that this war will close by spring that I can be with you agane and I think I can be contented to stay and let the nation take care of its self if I get home once more   I have but litle to write feel but litle like writing it and think some

times that I had ought to more but can not think what to write about I can tell you that cinc we left Roanoke we have found out what a soldiers life is   while there we lived a lazy life and did not know it but cinc we have had enough too do   we are still now and do nothing but oh what a diferance in the men we neve see a wrestle run or jump here while there it was comon   they wer at it all the time but here they lay in the tents all the time that they ar idle   it takes a good deal of time to get wood and keep our selves comfortable but the winter is mild for this plase and we have gaurded aganst cold all we can so we can live or rather stay   but I have got so tired of living in a pen like a hog that I look on the worst side of the picture and if it was not for thought that this war would close soon I should go crazy my thoughts by day and night are on home   it is the first thought in the morning and the last at night   I wish some times that I would think

---

[22] Lewis Sackrider, brother of Mary

of something els but it is all I know I feel that there is a great change in me and if I keep as I am you will heardly want to see me I fel cross and pevish and the boys find fault about it but I can not help it I hope I shall get over it if I have the good luck to get home agane as I do not feel comfotable my self and do not make others   but why wory you with this when I know that you have enough to bare at home   but oh may God grant that we may be together soon when we can tell each other our troubles and help each other bair them oh had I the wings of a dove but I can not write   my eys are dim so good by and may God bless and protect you and the children and grant us a spedy meiting is the prayer of your ever Loving husband

William A Robinson

Jan 19th 1863   This is headed: Camp Near Fredericksburgh

My Dear Mary
        I take this opertunity writing a fiew lines to you   I am well fat and ugly have nothing to do and am lazy to do it   I got yours of the 9th and 8th a fiew days ago and was glad to hear that Mother was geting beter and I hope she will keep geting beter   we re looking for pay every day now   they are paying some of the troops around us   I may send some money home and may not unless I hear of some

plase where it will earn somthing as I can do a litle with money here and make more than I use but use more than if I did not have it so pleanty   a dolar is worth about as much as 25 cts is there and I have got so used to it that it looks mo biger to me   I get the worth of my money in condenced milk of any thing I by   it cost 60 cts per lb and is worth about as much as 4 qts milk   it lasts about 10 days or 2 weeks to put in tea and coffee and makes dring that was not good quite palatable   I draw more sugar than

I want   it looks small to say 2 oz per day but that is over 50 lb per year and that will keep a family if each member gets it   it has been bery cold for 3 or 4 dayes back and this morning is a sneezer but I manage to keep comfortable in some way   I have drew a new over coat and the old one makes a good bed   I hav a good blanket that I drew in Elmira and a beter one that I captured of the rebels at south mountain and lent till we got here there is where I gained by a scarsity of cloths as Brown[23] could not get a blanket he was

glad to cary it till he could and not I have two they are large and I sleep with Dan Lee and Sol Butts and they each have one blanket the cover 3 quite easy and that makes 4 and two over coats and some old bags makes quite a bed and I slept as sound last night and as warm as ever I would wish to If I could come home Saturday nights and stay over sunday I could serve uncles Sam as well as any other man I had the blews when I wrote the last leter but it was not the first time and I spose it will not be the last you know how I act when

I get them and must not wonder at what I write I have no mony by me now or I would send some for fear you had not got to Delhi yet but I expect $40,00 day after tomorow as the man that I let it to will be here then and the rigiment that he is sutler to got pay yesterday if you hear of a chance to let a $100,00 let me know and I will make it out as soon as I can I can do it any day after we get our pay and have enough left to do all the buisness I will want to do here I have a watch that will bring $18,00 any time

about pay day and am writing with a pen and holder worth $2,00 more and the Co oew me $20,00 and there is $6,00 more that I do know but has gone to hunt the express bos that left NY the 15th of July as I sent it about 4 weeks ago and have not herd from it it makes $50,00 that I have lost in that way and I have lost about $20,00 more by bad debts and have spent a good deal and you know what I have sent home so you can see what I have made and every time that I loose I go to work to make

it up but the chance for making money here is slim at presant and if I make what I want to spend the rest of the winter I shall do well but I am geting tired and will have to close so good by and God bless and protect you and the children and grant us a pease is the prayer of you ever Loving Husband
                    William A Robinson

Jan 25th 1862[24] This letter is headed: Camp Near Fredericksburgh

---

[23] Hiram Brown, Pvt. Co. I
[24] This letter dated incorrectly, as it actually was written in 1863

Dear Mary
    I take this opertunity of writing a fiew lines to you   I am well and hope this will find you the same   we are still in the old camp and as lazy as ever   we have had an inspection to day as usual on sunday   the only way we know when it is sunday is we have more to do than any other day   I have nothing new to write   I had a leter from Frank and Wesley a few dayes ago   they wer all well we have had

a good deal of rain of late and the mud is worse than you ever saw or ever will see unless you should come to Virginia for it is the mudyest place on earth or any where else that I know of but the rain saved me from geting in another fight a fiew dayes ago and there is no danger of geting in one for some time to come in this place   I looked in vaine for a letter last night   I have not had one cince I wrote last but the paper is fool so good by and God bless you and the children is the prayer of your ever loving husban
                                    William A Robinson

February 5th 1863   This letter is headed: Camp Near Fredericksburgh

Dear Mary
    I recived a leter from you last night   it was the first in 3 weeks   I was glad to hear from home but was sory to hear that the children was sick but I hope that they are beter by this time and Oh how I would like to be home for a short time to see you all   I had some hopes of coming home this week but it is all nocked in the head now   there was an order for 2 men in every hundred to have a furlough and the Captain said he would do all he could to have me go home but when the time came he handed David Dixons name in and he will start tomorrow   I expect it is about the way the Captain fufulls his promises not only with me but all the rest   I think him the most double fast man I am aquainted with but I am in hopes that he will not have comand over me a great while longer for it seams to me that this war is about

played out for acording to the papers the north is about sick of this war and I know the soldiers is sick enough of it   they are diseriting by thousands here   ther has several gon out of our rigiment and a good many more talking of leaving and when it gets warm enough for men to lay out nights I think they will leave faster than ever   you nead not wory about my going hungry as we have enough to eat and a good deal to wast   and as for sufering with the cold we sit by the fire as much as we like but while one side burns the other is cold when it is cold weather but we have not had but a fiew cold spells and they only last a fiew dayes   I think this is the coldest snap we have had and I slept as warm last night as I could wish   I was down to the old maids monday and to see George Whitney[25] yesterday   I had a good time visiting both times   that is about all the way I have of taking comfort

I should not dislike soldiering so very bad if I could get home some times but this staying from home all wayes is more than I can stand and then to have incouragements of going home and have the captan turn round and work aganst me is all most to much for human induranc   you must tell Hanah and Daniel that I cannot write to them till it gets warmer as the tent is small and is full in cold weather so there is no chance to write

Tell mother that I think of her a great deal but have nothing to write that is interesting as there is nothing but camp life here and that is every day alike and a discriptsion of one day tell the whole story I am well and hearty at present   I think I am as well as I have been in a great while and if we do not make a moove I shall be as comfortable as a soldier has any right to be   and I do not think there will be a moove maid here till the last of March ar first of april

and by that time if maters keeps on at the north as they are going now fighting will be played out and God grant that it may as I have see enough   but I am tired of writing and will close so now good by and God bless you and the children is the prayer of you ever loving husband and the Loving father
William A Robinson

Feb. 10th 1863   This letter is headed: Newport News

Dear Mary

I take this opertunity of writing a line to you to let you know that I am well and hope this will find you the same   I am wating with anxiety to get a letter from you to hear how the litle boys gets along   we started from Camp Saturday morning and landed here Sunday night   it is now Tuesday and the first chance I have had to write   we are in log barocks and have inside bunk and are quite

---

[25] Pvt. Co. D of 101st NYV

comfortable we are a litle crowded and the nois is almost intolerable but I have got so used to hearing nois that I gues I can stand it if they will only let us alone while we are well off it is all I ask for the pesant the weather is warm and pleasant and we can play soldier here as well as we did at Roanoke The mail has just come and not leter from home but I supose you have all you can tend to and can not write but write as often

you can and I will try and be content I think you had beter direct as you have along back as we are lible to move any day some of the boys thinks that we are going to North Carolina agane but I think we was moved here to get beter quarters and that the army of the Potomack is all going to moove away from Fredericksburgh I have but litle to write and think I will close Jery got tight at Aquia creek and got left behind I will tell you when he get with us agane so now good by and may God in his mercy take care of you and the children and spare your lives if his will if not by Gods will be done
From your ever Loving husband
William A Robinson

Feb 15th 1863 This letter is headed: Newport News

Dear Mary
I agane take my pen in hand to write a line to you I recived yours finished the sixth two days ago and was glad to hear that the children was beter than when you last wrote I am well as usual and hope this will find you all well there is a great improovement in the boys cince we got hear they play ball and pich quoits and scuffle as they used to on Roanoke Jery got here about three days after us and looked as if he had had a genereal good drunk and was far from sober he wanted to borow $10,00 of me but I was short at the time and allways shall be at his call

I think you had beter caculate on staying where you are at presant if I should get home it will not take long to get a home of our own and I shall be as anxious for one as you

you said that mother wanted $50,00 I will let her have it if she will give you her note payable on or before the first day of January 1864 then if she gets her money for her buter she can pay it and if she does not get it by that time I will not hury her if I should get home any time I can get all the money that I want as severall fo the boys sayes they will be glad to let me have money I could borow

$1,000,00 if I wished to any pay day   there is $52,00 dues us the first of the month but I do not know how long before we get it   as soon as we get our pay I will send the money for mother
You need not wory about money that I have here if any thing should hapen to me as there is allwayes an arangement maid for you to get it
David Dixon did not get his furlo on acount of the moove and he tryed agane and Gen Dix would not sine it so he cant go   so Cap England shoed himself cheep
There was a man in a Conn Rigiment cut his throat this morning only a fiew rods from our barock   I do not think o any thing mort to write at presant so now good by and God bless and protect you and the children now and for ever is the prayer of you ever Loving husband
W A Robinson
P S
    Cap England has brought a galon of oisters for us and we are going to have an oister soop for diner   thing is cheep here to what they run at Fredericksburgh   oisters is 25 cts per qt   chees 20 cts per lb   buter 40 and cakes that 20 for 25 cts the same that sold 8 for 25 cts there   aples 11 for 25 cts
W A Robinson

Feb 23d 1862[26]   The letter is headed: Camp at Newport News

Dear Mary
    I take this opertunity of writing a fiew lines to you   I am well and hope this will find you the same   I recived yours of the 11th and 16th day before yesterday and was glad to hear that you had been to Delhi and got out of Janes cluches and I think that I will be as willing to keep out as you   we are having a good time here and hope it wil last but fear it will not   we had an afall storm yesterday and to day it snowed and rained and blowed tremendious but we thought ourselves lucky to be so well off   our barock is about as warm as your barn but it shelters us from the storm and I have saw as cold weather in april as it is here and as for sleeping I have a good bunk of cloths and sleep as warm as I could at home   I am geting fat as I was on Roanoke   I had a tooth puled to day and I thought the Dr would take my head off clean   You said you would send any thing I wanted by David or Jery if you saw them   it was the first time I heard that

---

[26] This letter is dated incorrectly, as it actually was written in 1863

Jery was coming home and I told you in the last how it was with David but I do not know as you could send any thing of benefit to me to pay the trouble   a grean back would not come amiss to me but I think I shall not send home for money unless I send some home and the rest of the boys gets from home and they all owe me so I manage to get enough to take comfort on   I had a good diner of oisters to day that suited me as well as any thing I could get if I was home   we draw a good loaf of bread evry day and you had beter believe it is a treat after the hard tack as long as we hav had it
You said you saw Case   did he say any thing of the $5,00 that Hunt let his wife have or had he pid it to Hunt

This paper is so mused that I can heardly write on it   I have no place to keep it but my knapsack and use that for a pilow and it muses my stationary bad enough but I gues I can live that through   I have about give up the war closing till our time is out but I think it will bother the Administration to get men in the place of the 300,000 that ges out in April and May and if they can not whip the south with them how can they with out
I hear that the 9 army Corps is to be a reserve to go where they shall be wanted   if that is the case we shall stay here for some time and if I could come home a while I would as live soldier here as do any thing   I can earn my money as easy as any where but I would like to see home once more   but I do not see muck of a chance at presant   I do not think of any thing more at presant so good by and God bless you and the children is the prayer of your ever Loving Husband
                    William A Robinson

March 2ond 1863   This letter is headed: Newport News

Dear Mary   I take this opertunity of writing a fiew lines to you   I am well and hope this will find you the same   I recived yours of the 22ond and 25 th to day and was glad to hear from you but sory to hear that there is so much sickness in the family   it seams as if some of you was sick all the time
   We are still hear and likly to stay for any thing that I see   we wer musterd for pay Saturday the 28 and I hear that the pay master is at the fortress wating for the pay roals and then will pay us our litle 52   I run against $4,00 to day quite unexpected and had an oyster stiew for diner and it bothers me to lean over to write   I have been promoted lately and perhaps you had beter be carful who you lets the children play with after this   I am Wagoner and the boys calls me mule

driver   I I get $14,00 per month and do the same duty as usual but if I drive I will get 25 cts per day extry but I think I see myself driving mules

at any price   we had a grand review a fiew dayes ago and it was a grand thing   the line must have been over a mile and a half long and they stood in divisions so there was 5 lines deep and in two ranks thier was about 15 000 men out   captain Englands father got here Saturday   he looks quite natural   but I do not think of any more to write so now good by and God bless and protect you and the children is the prayer of you ever loving husband
                               W A Robinson

March 9th 1863   This letter is headed: Newport News

Dear Mary
    I recived yours of the 3 and 4 to day and hasten to answer it   I am well and hope this will find you the same   I heard that we would get our pay on the 11th and hope it is true as I want a litle my self you shall have what you asked for and mor two as I do not want you to get out of money

J O Donell started for home day before yesterday on acount of sick relitives and doing his duty fathful for the past year and a half   I hope he will find them on the gain and keep sober and out of the guard hous while he is gon   do not send any thing by him if you had a chance as I do not want to risk a sents worth with him nor wish to be indebted to him

as soon as we get pay I will write agane and tell you where to find the money that I send   there is an order aganst a soldier pedeling so I supose I can not make any more money   I shall have to spend less or els I shall have but litle to send home   I do not know as I have any more to write so good by and god bless and protect you and the children

is the prayer of your ever Loving husband
                               W A Robinson

March 15th 1863   This letter is headed: Suffolk, Va

Dear Mary
I take this opertunity of writing a line to you   I am well and would be glad to know that this would find you the same   I have looked in vain for a lete from you all week and fear that you are worse   I have put off writing on two acounts   one was to hear from you and the other to see how we was coming out hear   the Rebs maid an atact on us Saturday and we have been schirmishing with them ever cince with small loss on boath sides   the 89th are in rifel pitts and are safe for the presant and reainforcements coming every day if the rebs want to try ther hand they will find a Fredericksburgh on the other hand as we are intrenced and ready for a muss   they will have to suround the plase

before they can get at where we lay and we are good fore four times our number when they get there   you must not get scared about me for I can stand hiking the works as safe as I could walk up to them as I have done before now   it will probably be some time before I shall get another chance to write but shall as soon as posable   I got a leter from the old maid monday   she was in a good humor and thought I was mad about what

she said about my coming home and made some handsome apoliges about it and said she ment that I was as worthy of a furlough as some of them that got one   that may be kising goes by favors here as well as other plases   but the paper is full so good by and God bless and protect you and the children is the prayer of your ever loving husband
William A Robinson

March 16th 1862[27]   It is headed: Suffolk, Va

Dear Mary
I imbrace this opertunity of writing a fiew lines to you   we moved day before yesterday and landed hear in the mud   are agane in hen coops without fire but by the time we get ready to moove agane we will have our tents raised up and look like live   Suffolk is a very prity place a litle larger than Bloomville on very level ground and the street is straight and brick walks on each side   there is three curches in it   one is a M E Church South   I atended that yesterday both Am and Pm   the paster preached in the foore noon and a

---

[27] This letter is dated incorrectly, as it actually was written in 1863

chaplain in the after noon   the second him in the fore noone was when I can read my titel clear[28] & the last was A charge to keep I have[29]   And when they began singing it minded me so of old times that tears came to my eyes unbiden and did not regain my composiour till after the servis was out   this was the first time I have saw the inside of church since I left Elmira and I can tell you it was a great treat   I hope I shall be able to go every sunday as long as I stay here

I am well hearty and hope this will find you the same   I shall look strong for a leter from you when mail come to night   we have not got our pay yet but Captain Cormack saw the pay master at Norfolk and he said we would be paid wednesday this week and would have had it sooner if it had not been fore the wagin

The mail had just come and a leter from you dated March 8th and 11th   I am sory to hear that you keep so unwell but that is all I can do for you at preasant   I want you to tell me how Jerymiah gets along at home and if he gets drunk on acount of sick relations   I will send money for mother and some for you as soon as posable when I get it I think you will have to send to the bank after it but will tell you more about it when it starts   I din not mean to write to Delhi and wonder how I maid the mistake but there was so much nois in the barooks that it would not have ben a wonder if I had done myself up and mailed and left the leter   I wish I had   but the paper is full so good by and God bless you and the children is the prayer of you ever Loving Husband   W A Robinson

---

March 23, 1863   This letter is on commemorative paper with a picture of a nurse tending a wounded soldier. It is headed: Suffolk, Va

Dear Mary

I take this opertunity of writing a fiew lines to you   I am well but been weighing only 162   We have had one of the worst storms this week that we have had cince I have been a soldier   the snow was about 6 inches deep and all slosh   when I got up one morning I found the

---

[28] The first verse is: When I can read my title clear To mansions in the skies; I'll bid farewell to every fear And wipe my weeping eyes
[29] A Charge to Keep I Have, words by Charles Wesley, 1762 from Leviticus 8:35, the music by Lowell Mason, 1832

water about 3 inches deep under me but I had put a lot of pine boughs under me so I was only deasantly damp   I went to town and sat down in a store and got by and felt like a new man and started to camp   I felt so spry that I went to jump a dich and fell in lengthways where the water was abut 1 foot deep   this rather took the feather edge of me for a while   I have got a bunk fixed in my tent now so I shall not get drounded out agane

I saw Jason Simmons yesterday for the first time in 8 years   he looked well and as naturl as could be   I new him when he was 10 rods off   he loocked so much like Charles   We get soft bread here that is just like home maid bread   what we get in other plases is like Baker's bread   this is the day I expect a leter from you   I will finish when the male gets in
   I got a leter from the old maid yesterda

Without a complaint or a fiew in it   only she thought I might come home as well as others   I answered it to day by saying I thought she might get maried as well as the rest of the girls   I could come if I could get a furlought and se could get maried if any one would have her   Jery got safe back but was glorious drunk   he got down and slept a while and then kicked up a nigar and ordered him to make a fire   then wanted to know how fare it was to

Suffolk and the next night he got led out dors by his nose   the felow that did it had a good hand full
   The mail has come and and no leter but I Think I shall get one tomorow night so I will bid you a good by and God bless and protect you and the Children is the prayer of your ever Loving Husband
               William A Robinson

March 26th 1863   This letter is headed: Suffolk

Dear Mary
        I take this opertunity of writing   fiew lines to inform you that I am well and hearty and hope this will find you the same   I recived yours of the 19th day before yesteday and was glad to hear that you was well   I should have answerd it yesterday but the Co was on picket which they have to do once in 3 days   the duty is to go to the river and lay around and do nothing   have to sit up 2 howers apice in the night and do nothing else but a loud roal call   so you see that I am not over worked   I got a leter from Wesley Saturday

with a pice of linen in it that Mary spun her first atempt   the newes of the fall of Vixburgh came here last night and confirmed to day this is an afall blow on the enemys and if rightly folowed up must break up the rebelion this sumar but I have lost all confidence in our leaders   Elder Jacobs arived here to day   I am in hopes that you will come and see me but leave it all to you   the stay here would not be very pleasant but the

sights you would see would repay you for all the trouble   if any thing should hapen that would make it in cosistant for you to come I will write   you would come in the cars to Baltimore and in a steamer to Norfolk and cars to Suffolk   no newes at prasant so good by and god bless and protect you and the children is the prayer of you ever Loving husband
                W A Robinson

April 2ond 1863   This letter is on commemorative paper depicting General Tyler's charge of March 23 at the Battle of Winchester. It is headed: Suffolk

Dear Mary
           I take this opertunity of writing a fiew lines to you   I have waited tw or three days to let the money get started   it started yesterday $60,00 for mother and you   we got our pay last saturday I got $56,00 or $14,00 per month for the last four months   I have got

nearly all the money fr the Co so I have pleanty by me for the presant and will try and not get out   I am well and hopes this will find you the same   I was on gaurd last night and feel to lazy to write muh   I got a leter from you the day after I wrote before and none since   I hope to get one to night

you will find the money at the bank   you had beter go after it yourself if not must send a writen order   it is directed
Inclosed sixty dolars
         to Mrs Mary E Robinson
              Kortright
From
      William A Robinson
      Co I 89th NYV
You had not beter go after it till after the 10th of Apr as it will take it

longer to get through than a leter   from your ever loving husband
            William A Robinson

Apr 20th 1863   This letter is headed: Suffolk

Dear Mary
        I take this opertunity of writing a fiew lines to you   I am well as ever and hope this will find you the sam   I recived you lettyrs of the death of Aunt Poly saturday and was glad to hear that you was beter   The 144th [30] arived hear friday and I had one of the best visits that I have had cince I left home and when I got back to camp I found your leter and one from Wesley   it maid me feel so good I could almost tast it   Lieu Thomas[31] asked me to remember him to you when I wrote   he has improved in looks cince I last saw him

I saw J Mc Kenry[32] but Jay Goodenough[33] was left liking to gaurd som suppl and had not got up yesterde   I saw all the rest that I was acquainted with   I took Hiram Simons[34] over to see his brother James[35] and they did not know each other   Yesterday was the aniversary of our first fight and of corse we had to have a good time so the 89th just steped over the river where the rebes had planted a batery and was raking our gunboats at a great rait and was so situated that we could not get guns to bare on them   so our boys just pounced on

them and took two 24 and three 12 pounders and 113 prisners   I did not go over as I hapened to be out of camp when the order cam   the 8 Conn went over with our boys to suport them and help hold what they got   our loss was two killed and about 12 wounded   none of Co I hurt   the Conn had one man drownd in giting off the boat   last thursday night there was a call for 50 of the 89th to go over the river and take some sharpshooters out of a house and burn the house and in less than half an hour ther was 50 vonunteer in line and started   Co I sent 15   I was one   we went over and run on a piquet

---

[30] 144th NYVI, raised in Delaware County, NY. Of special interest to Co I of 89th
[31] Lt. Dewill Thomas, Co. H, 144th
[32] James McKenzie, Pvt. Co. I, 144th
[33] Uriah J. Goodenough, Pvt. Co. H, 144th
[34] Hiram Simonson, Pvt. Co. H, 144th
[35] James Simmons (per muster rolls, despite diff. last name), Pvt. Co. I, 89th

line and got fired into and that alarmed the camp and spoiled the fun and we had to return   there was none hurt   we are having reinforcements any day and there is no likly hoods of the rebels making an atack on this plase   if they do they will suffer for there timerity   there is more or less skirmishing every day to the front and to heare canon is an hourly acurance but an in gaguement will not be fought here   I had the bad luck to loose $17 out of my pocket the other day but found $10 of it so I was only 7 out

(the next three pages are on commemorative paper depicting the "Great Battle at Pittsburgh Landing")

Mother and the girls are all well   Frank is still at Afton and Wesley sayes he thinks she will stay there   she and the old maid had a row over an old bed quilt which Sarah tryed to buy off but Frank out Generaled her and Wes likes up for the big side and sayes Sarah is not a welcom visitor at his house   poor old maid

I sent $10 in the last leter I wrote to you   I hope you have got it Jery says you have $200, in the bank   I would like to know where you got it and why you was so anxious for more   if you think of runing away with any on let me know and tell me how much it will cost and I will try and rais it for you as soon as posable and not keep you in suspense

Capt England has got his comishion of Liew Colonel and Co I presented him a spleandid sword saturday   The 144th are spoiling for a fight as they have not had a chance yet   they think it unfair to give us all the chance and we think so to   they can have my chance any time but I do not think of any more at presant that would interest you so good by for the presant and god bless and protect you and the Children is the prayer of you ever Loving husband
                     William A Robinson

Apr 27th 1863   This letter is on commemorative paper depicting the "Great Battle of Pittsburgh Landing", and is headed: Suffolk, Va

Dear Mary,
        I take this opertunity of writing a line to you   I am well and hope this will find you the sam   I recived Hanahs leter yesterday and was glad to hear that you had the money and was able to go to Delhi

we ar still in the rifel pits and like to stay there for a while as I see no hope of the Rebels making an

atact or easing the seage their visit her has stoped all furloughs and made the boys all mad and to quiet them the oficers gets up all sorts of storyes the last is that they ar trying to get a furlough for the whole rigiment for 60 days to come home and recruit I think they will git it but a military moove is slow and it will take about 17 months[36] unless the rebels should lay down their arms which might hury the mater some as for me I have give up all hope of geting home before fall

shall keep trying we have a new Captain England is Lieu Colonel Cormack is Captain of Co A and Lieu Nuton is Captain of Co I there is some talk of Cormack and Nuton changing but as they are boath nise men it makes but litle diferance I am going over to the 144th to day I send you in this a copy of the deads and wounded of the NY 89 it will be copied in all the Del Co papers and if you get hold of it in print save it I could have got it if I had have none it in time but it is to late now

The canon are booming her night and day but I can lay down and sleep as well as I could at hom and I gues beter than I should for a fiew nights I want to know howe the boys gets along in talking as it is like to be a long day before I shall hear them my self No more at presant so good by and God bless and protect you all is the prayer of your ever loving husband
     William A Robinson

May 5th 1863 This letter is headed: Suffolk

Dear Mary
  Thinking that you might hear of the batle of day before yesterday and be anixous about me I thought I would drop a line to you we had a first hot time of it we went ove the river and bearded the lion in his den the 89th and 103d NYV went in advance as skirmishers and had it about all to do we started at 8 oclock and was joined about noone by the 13th NHV and they behaved nobly we found the rebles in the woods and we had to meete them with no other

---

[36] Seventeen mos. was the length of remaining enlistment time for Co. I, 89th

covering but a rail fence and Co I used that to good advantage we wer orderd to get over the

fence and charde on the woods about 2 oclock and we did with a vengance Co I and I think Co G and one Co of the 13th when we got to the woods the rebels had buisness farther back and went to atend to it the only hurt I got was about noone I took a bitee out of my haversack and then went to take my regular smoke and stuck a sliver under my nale lighting my pipe the Dr thinks I will live it through we dusted the rebls down so they left that night and I think we will get some rest our Co had 3 men wound Lieutenan Epps back of the shoulder deep flesh wound

(the next page was on commemorative paper with a patriotic poem. The title and first line of a poem by WAR was written then crossed out)

John Thompson arm flesh wound John Davidson they stated cant live
The 144th leaves heer to day I am very sory to part with them
This is all the paper I have up from camp and to lazy to go after mor so good by and god bless and protect you and the children is the prayer of your ever Loving husband

W A Robinson

P S You can send the verses to Champ if you wish or keep them
W A R

May 11, 1863 This letter is headed: Suffolk It is on the same type of commemorative paper as the letter of April 27, 1863.

Dear Mary
I take this opertunity of writing a fiew lines to infor you that I am well and hope this will find you the same we moved back to camp the day I wrote you the last leter and changed camp agane yesterday we now have a nice camp with A tents set up on boards and good bunks and look

like keeping house the war news is chearing though I supose you hear the news as quick or quicker than I do the chance for a furlough is small at presant but they may begin to grant them soon agane and as we have a new Captain my chances is as good as any ones   I begin to hope that this war will close this sumar and let me home for good but it is hard to tell yet   The weather is very warm hear but as we do but litle that does not disturb me   I am fat and lazy and midling good natured

at presant   I got a leter from you last friday and was glad to hear that you was well and that Mother was well enough to get down to Hanahs you must tell me how Luis gets along with his work and I wld like to know how he behave to you and Mother and if you think you can stay where you ar all sumar without a fus   I do not know as I have any more to write at presant so good by and God bless and protect you and the children is the prayer of you ever Loving husband
W A Robinson

May 18, 1863   This letter is written on the same commemorative paper as described with the letter of April 27, 1863. It is headed: Suffolk

Dear Mary
         I recived a leter from you and one from the old Maid on friday she was well and quite contented for her   the leters was boath dated the 10 of may   the war news is not very good at prasant but not so bad as it looked a fiew dayes ago but when the end of the war

will come is hard to tell   our head men is incompetant or trators for they cirtanly have the means in their hands to crush this rebelion if they wer used to good advantage
I left George Avery[37] at Falmouth   his rigiment was composed of 2 years and 3 years men combined   the 2 years time is out some time this month   he did not know exactly whether he will git his discharge or not   I have not heard from him cince we left   he is not in the 9 army corps

Would you like to come hear and stay a month this sumar   if you would you can come if we are like to stay hear and we ar at presant but no chance for a furlough   if you could leave the children it would be beter as you could not hav the best of comfort here but I could get you a place near camp for a while   the cost would be

---

[37] George W. Avery, Co. D, 101st NYVI

about $25,00 and a prity hard ride   I do not know how you are situated to leave and leave it all to you whither to come or not

I acke all over to day with lazyness   we do not drill nor do any thing but gaurd duty and that is done at the halves   I am well fat and lazy sleep as much as I can read all I can get and lounge around the rest of the time   I must close for I am to lazy to write so good by and God bless you and the children
       From your ever loving Husband
           W A Robinson

May 31st 1863   This letter is on the same commemorative paper as the last letter. It is headed: Camp Near Norfolk

Dear Mary
       I recived a leter from you last night and was glad to hear that you was well but sory that you could that you could not come down hear   we moved last wenesday and have on of the most pleasant camps that we have ever had but

have to work on a fort 6 houres a day but there is one thing cirtain they will never hurt the 89th with hard work   I got a leter from Thomas a fiew dayes ago   his folks was all well
We are on the banks of the Elizabeth river and about 6 miles from Norfolk an for a wonder have camped on grass ground   we have our tents set up in a good order and look like live agane
I feal in a grat hury to hear from Vixburgh

it seams it was not taken when we heard it was but the last news we had was that it must soon surender   I think that when that is taken it will strike a damper on the rebls as it cuts them in two and gives us compleat controle of the Missippy river and I think will end the war this sumar
I am well as eve   no more at presant so good by and God bless and protect you and

children is the prayer of your ever loving husban
         W A Robinson

June 7th 1863 This letter is headed Camp Near Norfolk, va

Dear Mary
    I sit dow to day to speak a word to you   I am well and hope this will find you the same   we got our pay yesterday   I got $28,00 and sent $5,00 to mother to day   I shall not send any home unless you want it   let me know when you do

I have nothing to write to day   I send a pesant to Hanah   you will of corse all see it   I send each of the boys a picture and for fear you would not like one to make a bridge of your nose I send you also you see we have every thing neadful in the army and some things superfluous   I can not think of anything more and the orderly

just told me that I am on gaurd to day so good by and God bless and protect you and the Children and keep you safe from harm is the prayer of your ever loving husband
                William A Robinson

June 21 st 1863   This letter is very light, written in pencil. It is headed: Camp Near Norfolk Va

Dear Mary
    I recived a leter from you day before yesterdy and was glad to hear from you and that Charly was bater   I hope that the rest of you will not have the sore throat   I still continue in god health and am taking as much comfort as I can away

from home   we have ben fixing up our camp with pine bushes till it is nice   the Co is on two sides of a street and we have made an arbore the whole length of it in front of the tents with rude seetes to sit on so you can go out of one tent an in to half of the Co with out going in the sun and cross the street and go in

another arbore and go in the other half   we work just enough to keep us out of mischief and hardly that   the boys had a picknic last Wednesday and had about 25 or 30 ladies from Norfolk atended (of rather a doubtful carictor)   I was on gaurd at the dancing flour that night so I saw all the fun   it past off beter than we expected though the oficer of the day oficer of the gaurd Sargent of the gaurd and two gaurds to my notise

was gliriously drunk   I did gaurd duty when I had a mining and sit down when I pleased as there was no one to report me for non performints of duty   J O D was also on gaurd one of the two before mensioned   other ways he did very well as he had nothing to do with the ladies   there was some fault found with Co I because they had so litle to do with it   There is some talk of our going out on a short scout of 10 or 12 dayse soon so you

must not wonder if you do not hear from me in two weeks   I see by the paper that one of our rigiment that I was aquanted with was to be shot last friday for disursion and forgery   his name was Samuel Crumb of Co B and was drum major till just befor we left Roanoke when he was reduced for bad conduct   he diserted before the battle of south mountain   I had a leter from Wes Slusser friday   they was all well   Mother had been quite sick

but was smart then   it was writen last sunday   Jery and D. Lee and me went up the river about a mile and a half yesterday and rafted a lot of lumber and brought to camp by order   while waiting for the tides to turn we got sour milk for 10 cts per qrt and got a wench to make us som puding and we put ourserves around an enormus quantity in a short spase of time   No more at present so good by and God bless and protect you and the children is the prayer of you ever loving husband
          W A Robinson

June 26th 1863   This letter is headed: Yorktown Va

Dear Mary
          I take this opertunity of writing you a line to let you know that I am well   we reached here monday and I was agreeable surprised to recive a leter from you as I had one on Friday   I do not know when we shall leave hear or where we are going   am writing this in William Dibles tent   he is well and sends his respects to you   he gave me his likness and I send it to mother to keep her from crying becaus I did not send her a picture before   I am sory that you are so bothered and wood gladly do any thing to releave you   I think that we boath will learn to realise when we have a chance to take comfort by the time we get to gather agane   I think that if I wer in your place I should give the young man to understand that I asked no adds of him you can get som other place if you want to no mater if it does cost a litle more   I will live more savng and make up the diferance   you wanted to know how much I have

coming   I have two months the first of July   I have no money now that I can send you but shall have a litle as soon as we get back from this march which will be in a week or 10 dayes   as soon as I get it I will send you some   if you are in nead I can get 10 or 20 dolars any time and do not be bashful about saying that you want it   I could get it now but by the way that you wrote I thought that you was not in much of a hury   and now good by and God bless you and the children is the prayer of your ever loving husband
William A Robinson

July 10th 1863   This letter is headed: Yorktown

Dear Mary
    I take this opertunity of writing a line to you   we have had a hard march and got hear about an hour ago tired foot sore and dirty I am well and healthy   we have 20 miles to march yet and start in the morning   we will then go back where we started from   I hope to stay a while   as soon as I get there I will write the insidences of our march   it is a year ago to day that we left Roanoke and a hard year it has been but things look brighter than they did a short time ago I got a leter from you a fiew dayes ago and supose there is one in camp for me now   but I must write what I have a chance   good by and God bless you and the children
    Your loving husband
        W A Robinson

July 19th 1863   This letter is begun on a commemorative paper with a bust of "Corcoran" in the upper left corner in a patriotic frame, which has blanks for the writer to fill in for a heading. It is completed as: Camp Near Norfolk, 89 Reg't, Co. I, U.S.A., July 19th **1863**

Dear Mary
    I agane sit myself down to write a fiew lines to you   we arived safe in our old camp at Gettys point on tuesday the 14th found all things right and agane resumed our alteation at buisness and I will now give you a short scetch of our tramp   We started at daylight of monday I think it was the 27th and marched to Portsmouth 5 miles and shiped to yorktown and arived at night and stayed till the next morning after

I write to you from that place   then shiped to White hous landing about 22 miles from Richmond   the next day after arived the 144th came in on foot from Williamsburgh and I found Charly Stiles[38] among them   I also saw Alman Burows son at yorktown among the sick of the 144th and Al Simons also   they wer both giting beter and was around   we stayed several days at the landing and found a fiew vine black beryes to pick   they are a sweeter bury than the bush black bury   We wer got up at 3 oclock on the first of July and started on foot for Hanover Court hous

there was a large number of us   the whole of 3d division of the 9th army corps which is now the 2ond of the 7th army corps   the day was hot and owing to the ignorance of some of the Colonels some of the rigiments had there knapsacks with them   we had but our blanket and tent   we soon began to see blankets threw off along the road and in some places they wer in piles as larg as a hay cock   I have no doubt but ther was 2000 cast off worth an averag of $1,50 each   the next day we stoped about 10 oclock am and stayed till the next morning   while there I found a lot

of vine blackburyes   there was about one acre and it was a sight to see   it looked like a black spot of the sise   there was bushels of them as large as you thumb and swee as you ever saw   I eat all I could and filed my cup and cap in les than a half hourer   I had just 3 quarts when I got to camp   there must have been 5 bushel in our rigiment that night and I know not how many in other rigs   the next morning day light found us on the marce and it was 10 at night before we stoped   in the morning we found

another bery pach and did it justis   I got 2 qts wer all I could eat about 10 ocock we wer ordred to roal and pack our blankets and get ready to march   this looke like fight as we was near Hanover and leaving blankets is not comon on a march and as it was the 4th of July we expected to have a grand celabration but got disipointed as we got to Hanover without seeing but 5 rebles and them we captured   we camped at Hanover that night without blanket or tent   ther was a feild of whet there just cut and that made a bed   by the way we had wheet for a bed every night before and tent and blanket to boot while we stayed there the 11th Penn cavelry and the 99th NYV tore up the rail road for about 12 miles and did other damage to hinder

---

[38] Charles Stiles, Pvt.Co A, 144th

reanforcements from giting to Lee   the next morning we started on our way

back   I was taken with a diareah and got the Dr to put my gun and cartrige box in the wagon   that left me nothing to cary and I got along first raight   we took a diferent road home and marched till one oclock in the morning and the bagage did not come up so we had the soft side of mother earth for a bed and a stary sky for a covering that night and no straw but I never slept beter   the next day I was beter we made but a short march and had wheet blanket and tent that night and well for us for it rained great guns   another bery pach here and I got 1 qrt   the next day we started I took my gun and traps   the Dr said I had beter leave my blanket and tent with him and I did and picked up another and sold it the next morning for 50 cts so you see I was in a living condition   thusday brought us back to the landing but a misery our march

was not ended yet for the next day we was ordered to start on foot for yorktown which took 3 dayes more hard marching   the night was rainy and the next day we started on our march acrost a swampy pease of wood land about 3 miles acrost and any one that had never been in the old Virginia low lands can form no idea of the mud we had to got through and to help the mater about 2 oclock it rained tremendious we stoped a while after we had got well drenched and put up our tent and just as we got taking comfort we was orderd to start   blankets tents and clothes wet and not very light to cary but night came and a halt also   the next night we in camped in bout 50 achers of black buryes and the picking was good and pickers pleanty for over 12000 men had all they wanted that night and pleanty in the morning   the next day was lightened as we thought that

our marching wood close that night cirtin but how rong our hopes we got toYorktown about 3 oclock to hear that we must march to Fortress Munroe 24 miles further and I wrote you a leter that night expecting to start in the morning but good nature got the beter of General Getty and he let us lay over the next day and rest   we went in the bay to bathe and one genious found clams there and we went to fishing and eating   the way we got them was go in the water up to our neck and dig the clams out of the sand with our toes and then dive and get them   I got 100 and clam soop was the ord of the day   the next morning marching was resumed and at about 2 oclock we stoped as we had got over half way   we staid on the batle field of Big

Bethel vine black buryes had played out but bush buryes had begin to ripen and I got a good suply

the next morning we was up before day and on the march arived at Hampton about 10oclock this was once a prety place but was burned down by (?) after the batles of Big Bethel this was where we was to stop so our march was over but we could not get transportation till the next day we got to Portsmouth about 10 oclock and had 5miles to march in the heat this brought us back to our old camp and we broke ranks with one tremendous yell glad to get back for we wer tired and foot sore and some dirty as we had not had a change of close since we left which was 3 weeks and 1 day we found all things about as we left them

but my knapsack had got damp and about spoiled all my paper and the blanket that I left was quite moldy The place that I saw while on the march shoed the marks of war plane Yorktown is what the sotherners calls a right smart town it would take 4 such place to be as large as Bloomville but is in the center of a large fort the largest that I ever saw except Munroe Hanover is a corthous jale and tavern there is a rail road station about ½ mile from it but only the buildings nesesary to cary on the buisness A(?) is about large as Bloomville and nearly half burned down King William is about halfe the sise Williamsburgh is about as large as Delhi Hampton about the sise of Bloomvill White House

landing is a landing for steam boats conecting with a rail road it takes its name from the hous that Washington was maried in but has been burned since the war comenced the plantation is ownd by William Henry Lee an oficer in the confederate army I am well as ever and think I have saw enough on the march to pay me for all the work and would be willing to take another jaunt if nessary I supose you have heard of the row in NY I would like to be ther with the rest of the 89 I think we could stop it prity quick it will prolong the war if it is posable to prolong it but the fall of Vixburgh and Port Hudson cuts the rebls in to and leaves them but a smal hope if they suckseded in capturing Lee it would have put and end to the thing at

at once but if there was no treason in the north this war would close in 2 months and I think it must close this fall anyway But I am geting tired so good by and God bless and protect you and the children is the prayer of you ever Loving Husband

William A Robinson

July 25 1863   This letter is headed: Camp Near Norfolk

Dear Mary
    I agane set myself down to say a few words to you   I recived yours of the 19th yesterday and was very glad that you are as well as you ar   I had not had a leter from you befoer since I was at Big Bethel 2 weeks ago tomorrow tho it seems but yesterday   the time flyes on swift wings with me   it does not seam a month cinc I was on Roanoke Island though what a sight I

have passed through cince   the time pases faster than ever here   I take as much comfort as I could anawhare away from home   I can pick bereyes when I like play ches dominoes or checkies till I get tired sleep when I have a mind and work enough to give me an apetite and still find time to write when not to lazy   the weather is such at presant that one would want to lay off theer fleash and sit in their bare bones and then would not be coole without punching out the midraf to give the air a chance

to circulate but I can stand hot weather as well as a salamander   my flesch is so solid that the boyes sayes that I am all bone   I have not heard from Wes or the old maid in a long time   I supose that they are waiting for a leter from me   I shall write to them this afaternoon if not to lazy
    We expect to be filed up with drafted men as soon as they can be got here   then we will have to drill to give them a chance to learn it will take about 700 to fill us up

I do not think of anything more that will interest you so good by and God bless and protect you and the children is the prayer of your ever loving husband
                William A Robinson

July 31st 1863 This letter is headed: On board ship Adalade Of Cost of South Carolina

Dear Mary
    Well they have Just went and gon and don it now   they have sent us away down south most close to the moone   we was waked

up in the night to tell us to be ready to march at an early hour in the morning   we was ready by 10 oclock and marched to portsmouth and stayed there till one the next morning then shiped and stayed till daylight and started for we knew not where

but we begin to mistrust that our destination is Charlston harbour   I am well fat and lazy   they boys say they neve saw me look as fat before and a sea ride neve disagrees with me   I have saw lots of flying fish to day but nothin els to mension   I have nothing more to say at presant so good by and God bless you and the children is the prayer of your ever Loving husband
          W A Robinson

August 15th 1863   This letter is headed: Folly Island S C

Dear Mary

    I agane take my pen in hand to say a fiew words to you   I am not very well at presant nor very sick about midling   feeal beter to day than for 3 dayes back and gues I am going to get well   the Dr sayes he has the advantage of me for the medicin is so bad tasted that I had rather get well than take it and he is about right   it has cost me from 2 to 3 dolars per day to git stuf to eat and haint eat much at that but drink goes

down easy   I have drank from 5 to 6 qts of tea per day and paid $2,00 per pound but was good tea   I want you to take the diper and go to the spout and take one long strong pull for me   I had a long story to tell about the ocien and the treas but will put it off once more and perhaps weight till I see you and till it   Jay Goodenough and J Mc Kenzie are on this island   I have not saw them yet but will when I get beter   they came about 4 days ago   I want you to tell me all about the boyes

if they are good and if they improove in talking   no more at presant so good by and god bless and protect you and the children is the prayer of you ever loving husband
          William A Robinson

Aug 23d 1863 This letter is headed: Folly Island, S C

Dear Mary

I recived yours of the 30th yesterday and was glad to hear from you I have got well agane and feal stout and hearty   you wanted som money   I can not send it from hear   I do not expect this will leave hear in a week or 10 dayes   I supose the last that I wrote is yet at Hilton Head   I supose you will ear about catipiler before you hear from me but I can not help it   I can write but can not hury the mail if you lack money when

you get this go to Bloomville and git some of Champ and write to Aron Hunt and ask him to send you what you want   then pay Champ tell Hunt that I will send some as soon as there is a chanc which will be soon   there is $58,00 due me from the government when we get pay ther will be a chance to send home by express   I got a leter from Mary and Frank yesterday   they wer all well but mother she was not very well but I have but litle time to night and can wright agane by the

time this will leave   Jay Goodenough was killed while on picket on the night of the 15 or 16 by a shell from the rebls   good by and God bless you and the children and tell charly that I will come home one of thes fine dayes and beak Liusis nose if he bother him
       William A Robinson

Sept 13th 1863 This letter is headed: Folly Island, S C

Dear Mary
    I now take my pen in hand to write a fiew lines to you I am well at presant and hope this will find you the same   I have been attached to work on some ovens and work 8 hours a day and dont grunt   the job is a most done and I am sorry for it seams so nice to be at work agane   I mean to try and get another job if I can   I will tell you next time how I make out   I send you one dolar make good use of it   it be the last you get   I have not done much at what I spoke of in the last leter   I find the mail goes regular   I will send you a dolar a week for a fiew weeks   I have been in the Ocin to bathe to night and a right good time I have had   the breckers roal high and one moment the water is about wast high and the nex one is caried high up in the air or roaling in a raving flood that roals him about in all direction

but I am tired and I gues I close   I like to for got that we was disapinted to day and got our pay before we looked for it and I

have sent $50,00 to the bank for you   it is subject to your ordr and you had beter let it alone till you want it   keep coole about it being there and get that mony of Hanah if you can by neading it   get alitle at once   I will trust a dolar at a time as long as I can aforde it and when you must have it send to the bank and get it   No more at presant so good by and God bles and protect you and the Children is the prayer of your ever Loving husband
William A Robinson

Sept 19th 1863   This letter is headed: Folly Island

Dear Mary
    It is now two weeks cince I have had a leter from you but expect the male to day or tomorow and then perhaps I shall get two to make it up   I am as well as comon and hope this will find you the same   We do not expect I D Jacobs[39] to live from one hower to the next   I have just writen to his father   it was a hard job but must be done   I have writen twice before cince he has been sick   I am still where the work is but the work has stoped and I am doing nothing only watching for a chance to stay   I have the promis and will stay as long as we remain in this department if the Capt does not head me off which he will if he can but when a man once gets out of a Co it is easy to keep out and I shall wach my

chance as it is mor pleasant to sleep nights than stand gaurd
    I send you a york state bill   it cost me 25 cts   I think it good try it and see   let me know whither it pases or not   I do not think of any thing more that will interst you so good by and God bless you and the children from your ever Loving husband
William A Robinson

Sept 27th 1863   This letter is headed: Folly Island

Dear Mary
    I take this opertunity of writing a fiew lines to you   I am as well as common and hope this will find you the same   I got yours of the 8 and 9 to day and was glad to hear from you but sory to hear that aunt was sick   I have not saw James[40] since he came here   he is about 3 miles from me but it is dificult to get a pas here   we are

---

[39] Ira Jacobs, Sgt. Co. I, 89th
[40] James McKenzie of 144th, a step-cousin of Mary Robinson

about 5 or 6 miles from Charlston but canot see the city   I have all the names of the drafted in the county   I see a great many that I am aquainted with   Jim Bears is among the number   I expect to send this by Charles Freibig who is going home on a furlough soon   I have nothing of any acount to write so good by and god bless and potect you is the prayer of you ever Loving husband
      W A Robinson

Oct 3d 1863   This letter is headed: Folly Island S C

Dear Mary
 I agane take my pen in hand to inform you that I am as well as usual and hope these fiew lines will find you and the boyes well   I do not think I can spare any more money till next pay day which will be by the 15th of next month   I do not hear from you only about once in two weeks of late   I do not know whether it is because the leters are lost or becaus you are to busy nursing to write   I have sent on every week cince I have been on the Island and would like to know if you get all them   I have sent a dolar bill in towo of them   on a greenback the other a state bill   did you get them   if you want money go to the bank and get it   if not let it be there till you do want it   I shall send more as soon as I get pay agane

I have not news to write   there is nothing going on here and nothing to see but sand and water and the implyments of destruction so good by and God bless and protect you and the children is the prayer of your ever loving husband
      W A Robinson

P S
 If you wright Volunteer in full on the back of the leters spell it right
    W A R

Oct 16th 1863   This letter is headed: Folly Island

Dear Mary
 I gues you begin to think I have forgoton you but the vesel sailed last week a day soner than usual and I was not ready and there was no use in writing till it sailed agane   I am well as usual but have not been very well cince I came hear   I get lots of good water for the last week anc can get it as long as we stay hear as I have maide

friends with some felows that get it of the sanatary comision and I have all I want   the rest of the boys drink Island water   I recived yours of the 25th yesterday and one from frank[41] that I inclose as the news may be interesting to you   I have nothing to write but the same old story so good by and God bles and protect you and the children is the prayer of your ever loving husband
William A Robinson

Oct 24th 1863   This letter is headed: Folly Island

Dear Mary
   I recived yours of the 11th just now and was glad to hear from you   I recived yours of the 27th the next day after I wrote my last   You wanted to know about Bob Zeah   he diserted soon after the batle of Antietam and we have not heard of him cince   I think he joined a batery of regulars as he siad he ment to the first chance he got   Jacobs died the day I wrote you that he was sick   I supose you have heard of it long ago   the rest of the Co are well   he had the bloody disentary   I have not been to the 144 as they are some way of and we are on duty almost all the time   I am glad you payed Elick   it is so much off my mind   I hardly know what to say about leting Aunt Rhody[42] have 25,00 for a year as I shall want all the money that I have when I get

home where I can use it if I want to and I can not tell when I shall get home   I would like to have all the money earning something if I could but rather not let it longer than the first of may at presant and would like to acomodate Aunt if posable and upon the whole I think she is safe and you had beter let her have it as I think if I want money when I get home I can get it of the boys that will be glad to let it   but I should not like to let any more for a year   I had thought that if Mother got along well this sumar and was like to do well and wanted to keep that 50,00 till another fall I should let her but perhaps she had beter pay half of it and let Aunt have the other but if she realy wants it let her have it and Aunt to for ther notes will raise more for a short time without seling them as money will be pleanty when the war closes   you neade not tell Mother just

---

[41] This letter from Fannie (Frank) Robinson, sister of Wm. was in fact saved by Mary, and the "news" was notice of the marriage of their sister Sarah Robinson, the "old maid" of earlier letters
[42] Rhoda Goodenough McKenzie, a maternal aunt of Mary Robinson

what I have said but act your own judgement about the mater   you can tell whether eather her or Aunt is safe or not beter than I can and the most is to get the money back some time   if Mother does not want it any longer and you can lets it safe till the first of May let it go but no longer till you hear to the conterary from me   I do not feel very well to day but think I shall be beter soon   tell Hanah and Dan if they want to know about Jery they must coraspond with him   I did not tatle when I was home and do not mean to hear   no more at presant so good by and God bless and protect you and the children is the prayer of your ever loving husband
                    William A Robinson
There was no stamps in the last 2 leter and this is my last one

---

Nov 28th 1863 This letter is headed: Folly Island S C

Dear Mary
     I recived yours of the 11th the last male and had Just finished reading it when one of the boys brought me one of the 19th with 6 stamps in it   I was glad to see them as I was out having used the last on the lete I had just writen you   you had beter send about 2 every time you write then I would have enough for myself and som to spare a frind som times but it won't be to small to speculate

on   my health is much improved of late and I feel well to day and hope this will find you as well   you seam to think if I have not enought to do here I had beter leave   that would be jumping out of the frying pan into the fire as there is nothing but gaurd duty to do in the Co and that is siting on a log 2 hours out of six for on 24 hours and nothing to do the next while here I do have a pail of water to fech once in two days and now and then some other chore to do about eaquel

I wish our work was a litle more eaquel divided but so it is in this world   we must take things as they come and remember that it is but litle over 9 months mor before we can have our own wey once more I heard from J McKinzy yesterday   he was well but I must close as ther is a job to do fixing the tent so good by and God bless and protect you and the Children is the prayer of your ever loving husban

                    W A Robinson

Dec 3d 1863   This letter is headed: Folly Island S C

Dear Mary

I agane sit down to say a fiew words to you   I am giting beter every day   I have returned to the Co   you wanted to know when I thought this war would end   I think by spring but it is hard to tell but 9 and a half months will end my part any way so have good cheer   we got our pay last sunday and I had the luck to loose all mine and some more with it   I lost $32,00 but shall have enough left to

spend till we get pay agane but I may not send any to you till 4 months from now so look out for your self but if any thing should hapen that you want mony I can let you have it   I am sending for a set of tools that I can make something with   they are to cut leters to mark cloths with which is wanted very bad in the army   I have the money to pay for them but I borowed it   if they come all right it is likely I can send my next pay home but if not I cant   I expect Dixon[43] to fech this to you

We expect a male to morow then I shall look for a leter from you and will be glad to get it   I could come home this winter if we had a Captan that was fit to comand men but he ant and I never will gite down on my marow bones to a man or boy and with out I do not expect much favors of him but he neve abuses any on so he is not so bad as he might be but if I keep as well as I am now I can stand my time out for months seam like weeks with me

I do not think of any more to write to night so good by and may God wach over and protect you and the children and grant that we may agane meet in this world if not may we meete in heaven   from your ever Loving Husband
                    W A Robinson

P S do not try to send any thing by Dixon as he will have all he can fech and I do no nead any thing that you can send
                    W A Robinson

Dec 4th

---

[43] David Dixon, Co. I, 89th

the male has come and a leter from you with 2 stamps in it and one from Wesley   he sayes salt peter won save him from the next draft   Sarahs husban is in the army and near Washington   I send you $5,00 in this and will send you as much mor next pay dy which will be in less than two months   I am welll and hearty and giting fat good by
W A Robinson

Dec 13th 1863 This letter is headed: Folly Island S C

Dear Mary
    I recived a leter from you day before yesterday and was glad to hear from you dated Nov 29th   I am sory that you do not feel beter this winter   I am well but tired to day   I was on gaurd out of camp last night and it rained hard all day and I got wet   then 3 of the boys out of 6 got to drunk for duty and I was up about all night   this would give them 6 houres a day for 8 days double quick on a surcle

if reported but they was good boys and would not report me if I got in a scrape and would do as much to healp me out and such times helps to pass off the time   we had a high old time lafing at them this morning
    It was a year agot to day that we marched up to the wall at Fredericksburgh and it   I am tired and the day is stormy   I take some more comfort than I did that day   I have a good fire place to sit by and it feels good to day though it is not cold but

I was wet through this morning   the fire place is one of my own building   it is made of swamp sods and a good chimny of the same toped out with a baril   I bought the baril fool of aples and eat all I wanted and sold the rest for a dolar more than I gave   the dolar bought me 2 ½ lb buter which will last me about 2 weeks so you see I live at home   we have good bread and I toast it and live on toast and tea but I must close so good by and God bless you and the children
                  W A Robinson

Chapter Three
Letter Transcriptions 1864

Jan 2ond 1864 This letter is headed: Folly Island

Dear Mary
    I take this opertunity of writing a line to you   I have not heard from you in two weeks and do not expect the male till monday I hope then to get good news then   I am well and giting fat every day   last night was the coldest night we have had this winter and I had to turn out at 4 oclock this morning and stand gaurd till 8 but all I had to do was keep warm   I have

toasted my shins by the fire the rest of the time to day   it has not thawd all day and to night will be a singer   there has about 30 or 40 of the 89th reenilsted but only two out of Co I and one of them was not me   I gues I shall get enough by the time I git out now   if I do not it will be time enough when I git out but it is giting late so good by and god bless you and the children   from your ever loving husband
                W A Robinson

Jan 10th 1864 This letter is headed: Folly Island S C

Dear Mary
    I now sit down to say a fiew words to you   I recived yours of the 18th last tuesday and was glad to hear from you   I am well at pesant and hope this will find you the same   it is cold here yet   it frose hard last night and is cold today and I am toasting my shins by the fire and thinking that it is the last winter in the army as the $1000 dolar bounty will not by me   I told them that if I could go

home and talk the mater over with you and we boath agreed to it I wood inlist but if you agreed to it they could bet there boats I wood not   ther is 7 of Co I reenlisted   ther names is H Brown of Davenport S Butts of Croton W Stott Washington D C R Dyer Delhi vilage J Wight Delhi W Rivenburgh Walton W Blinby Chenango Co   there has nearly 100 in the rigiment and leaves about 100 more able doded men   the vetrens expect to start for home the 15th of this month on a 30 day furlough so you see if I had been one of them you woold sooner see me   I think the reinlistment will break up the rigiment and am in hopes to be discharged soon after the first of Aprill and ther is talk that the call of 300 000 that came out first will be discharge the first of July but the 16 of September is the longes that they can hold me anaway and the prospect for a close of the war is prity fair at prsant so taking the mater all in concideration I think the time will soon roal round when I shall get home to

Stay   I do not think of any thing more to write to day so good by and God bless you and the children is the prayer of your ever Loving husband
        W A Robinson

P S I want to know what Hanah wants of you this winter   it looks suspisious to me   It was a mistake the last leter going with out a stamp
        W A R

Jan 22 1864 This letter is headed: Folly Island S C

Dear Mary
    I agane sit down to say a fiew words to you   it is Just 2 years and 3 months since we left Delhi and it does not seam half that time and if the other 8 months goes as fast as the time that has past it will not seam long till I shall agane be home   they are still reaninlisting in the rigiment   I think they will break up the rigiment by the first of march   there has 2 inlisted cince

I last wrote in Co I   I did not get any leter the last mail and made up my mind that you might be buisy douting Hanahs young one in return for her kindness in doing the same for you   but you must not let the thing bother you so much that you can not wright to me or I shall not give it a new dress when I get hom   I would get it one right away but I think that it will not grow as fast as calico will go down so I shall make by waiting   if it is a boy call it William Alfred   if a girl Fannie

Angeline and I will warent it a sheep   I still keep well and hope this will find you the same   the wether is rainy the most of ther time excep when it lets up to freeze but winter is sliping away fast as the spring opens here in February   I was down to the 144 yesterday and found the boys all smart   I did not see Jim   he was to head quarters on gaurd and it was to far to go   I took diner with Eugene Thomas and had som of Mrs Thomas buter and it tasted like home it was the first buter I have had cince I left

home that was good   ther was a fight among the prisoners to day one lost a finger and the other an eye so it was a prity even thing   no more at presant so good by and God bless and protect you and the children is the prayer of your ever loving husband
                    W A Robinson

I had just seald this when I got yours of the 27 to the first of Jan   I sent a leter by Dave Dixon with $5,00 in it and hope you ha got it befor you get this but I supose he is so buisy with his luck that he does not think of any thing els but he will get around after a while he promised to write back but not a word have we herd from him yet I have given my mind on inlisting before but if any one tells you that I will inlist tell them I can not see the point

I told the oficers that if they would send me home and let talk the maters over with you and if we bothe cold agree I would inlist but if you greed they could bet their life I would not for I have been hounned by sholder straps about enough
                    W A Robinson

Jan 25 '64 This letter is headed: Folly Island SC

Dear Mary
         I agane wright a fiew lines to inform you that I am well and hope this will find you injoying the same blessing   I recived a leter from you wednesday dated up to the 6th and was glad to hear that David had sent that money to you at last   I think he might be ashamed of him self as he promised to send it right away if he could not go down and see you   he also took another leter for me that I have not herd from yet

ther was $20,00 in the other   I have made $25,00 cince I lost my money which nearly pays up all I borowed   we expect pay soon and I shall send you what you want as I shall not have use for any my self   You say you do not see why I do not git a furlough   do you not know that kising goes by favors as well in the army as any where else and I neve was good at nosing around those that thought themselves beter thatn me but it is giting along   so now that I do not feel as much like wanting one as I did

and we are having nice time now compaird to what we had a year ago living as diferant as day and night   we have comfortable tents with fire in and good living by paying about $5,00 per month   we can live as well as we could at home and as for duty we do not have enough to keep us out of mischief   if I could get home as often I should prefer this buisness to laying wall but I think I shall have enough by the time I get out without reinlisting   I send 50 cts in this for the benefit of that wonderful new comer

as he has taken a cold dreary time to visit a cold dreary world   I think a small presant will not come amiss at any time   Hanah must git what he most needs with it and tell his his soldier uncle sent it and he must be a good boy and mind his Pa and ma till I come home and if he is handsom I will give his a candy and if named as directed in my last he shall have a sheep before he is a year old or else I will be uncle the sod   there is a man in our company making me two

picturs for my boys   one is done now and it is handsom to   the other will be ready by the time I shall wright agane so they will get them both to gather   I do not think of any thing more excep Eugene Thomas is up her and he looks fat and healthy   so good by and God bless and protect you all is the prayer of your ever Loving Husband
       William A Robinson

Jan 30th 1864   This letter is headed: Folly Island S C

Dear Mary
  I recived yours of the 10th and 13th to day and was glad to hear from you   I also got a leter from Wesley and one from Mrs Sarah P. Astin   I cant say the old made any more   I also got a buyseness leter in answer to one that Dixon took when he went away and I was glad to hear from it as there was $20,00 in it and I began to think it lost   if Dixon fulfills his promise to his Duck as he

has to Co I may God forgive him for he never can but I do not wish to tatle so I will stop here
 I think that if you should look in on me some night you would be surprised to see how I live   as for caciching me smoking it was very litle that I smoked from the first of August till the middle of January some times not once in 2 weeks but I   have begun latly and supose I

shall get as bad as ever before I get home
   About your geting a new home   I will think about it and tell you next week what I think

we will git our pay in the morning   I expect James Wight to see you when he comes home and he will fech you the money   He may fech this leter but is not shure of coming this week   I shall send a pipe that I bought in Anapolas and smoked in on 3 batle fields also a tape line that I captured in Fredericksburgh   you can put them with the rest of the prity things that I have sent home
Frank was in New York when Wes wrote   he is going to Iowa in the spring to live and Mother is going back

city   my tent mates is George Stott and William S Law   Charles Siliman is in the invalid Corps and W Drumond is with us well and tuff   As for making money that is just as it hapnes when there is a chance I go in   I sent for stensil tools by Dixon and should have make a good thing of it if he had mailed the leter at NY as he should it may be two weeks yet before they get here as they did not start till the

13th of this month when they should have started the 15th of last month   Sarah wrote me a mess of love sick trash worse than a 16 year old moone struck girl would write to a truant swane and finished by growling about the way the other girls used her   I beleave she is more of an old made cince she got maried than before but then she is like a grass widow as her man is in the army   I send the pictures I spoke of in this

the man that made them is the nicest man in the Co   he is a christian and about 40 years old   he belongs in the town of Tompkins   his name is Anderson Gaston   I gave him 25cts for his trouble   The weather has been pleasant here the last week about like corn planting weather   I am writing to night without a fire and am warm enough my tent mates ar boath on gaurd so I have the whole swing of the tent not more at presant so good by and God bless you and the children from your Loving husband
          W A Robinson

Feb 9 '64   This letter is headed: Folly Island S.C.

Dear Mary

I now take my pen in hand to inform you that I am well and hope this will find you the same   I recived yours of the 24th last night after I was in bed   I was glad to hear from you and if Dan is mad let him scrach his --- and get over it   you can live with out him as well as he can with out you I recon

I do not see as these men that has reinlisted ar like to get home very soon   I ment to send som money by J Wight

and some other things but I do not see as he will get there very soon I send you $5,00 in this and will send more some day

My stensil tool have com and I have got about $5,00 of the 20 back that paid for them   I have you name and would send it in this but as there is money in it I think I had beter not but will send it soon   if Wight coms I can send a brush and ink two

About your giting a new hom   I do not know what to say   I have but litle hopes of geting home till the first of July

and no cirtenty till the 16 of september and you would not like to stay alone till I get home but if you can not stand it where you are look up som other place to board for I can find a home some whare when I get there   If you can find a house that would not cost over $15,00 per year you had beter ingague it from the first of May and then act your pleasure about mooving in   I would like to get Langlies shop if I could   that and Widow Thomas hous is all that I know of in that neiborhood   you might find out if you could get eather

if you ingague a hous be shure and pay $5,00 dow then they can no let it agane if you did not moove in at wons but I would not live in Jim Sackroder hous if he would pay me $25, a year   you might speak to John Peters but do not hire a hous of him with out first writing to me no more at present so good by and God bless you and the children from your ever loving husband
                      W A Robinson[44]

Feb 13th 1864   This letter is headed: Folly Island S C

Dear Mary
               As the vetrans start to day I shall send a line to you by Wight   I have no time to do any thing as the news came in the night

---

[44] The name this time is stenciled with the new kit instead of written, as was the address on the envelope

and they start at 9 oclock   I am well and hope this will find you the same   we look for the male to day   I am out of stamps   I send you a brush and ink but the plate with your name on is out of camp but I will send it in a leter   Wight will let you have as much money as you

so take enough to last you til the midle of may   I have to go on gaurd at ½ past 7 and a good deal to do so good by
William A Robinson

Feb 24 '64   This letter is headed: Folly Island SC

Dear Mary
    I take this opertunity of writing a fiew lines to inform you that I am well and hope this will find you the same   I recived yours of the 30th and 2ond last sunday and was glad to hear that you was well I should like to know what you are about up north to raise such a breeze   it come down two dase cold as a step mother's breath and strong as a lovers quarel   it walked in to my bones like an

acomplished burgler in a rich mans house   I was on gaurd yesterday and felt all day as if the hand of misues charity was layed on my back it froze ice in a cup on my table with a good fire in the tent but it is warmer to day and likly to get warmer
    Charly want to know what I did sundays   I have been on gaurd for the last three sundays and was notifyed that I could thare the same plasure tomorow   I thought to escape last sunday when I was writing the leter that I sent by Wight but the order

was changed and insted of going as gaurd that day I was on sunday
    I hope that Wight will see you before this reached you but if not tell him just what maney you want and he will let you have it but take all he has of min   if you do not want it you may want $5,00 to pay a quarter rent if you should hire a hous and it will be the first of May befo you will have a chnace to get any mor from me
    We expect a male tomorow and may it fech news from home

I waked up the other morning rather cross for I dreamed that I came down the hill by D Thomasas and came in sight of home   I began praising my self that I was home and it was no dream this time such as had cheated me so many times and than waked up and found my self in my tent   but I can not aford but one sheat of papaer so good by and God bless you and the children is the prayer of your ever loving husband

       W A Robinson

March 13th 64 This letter is headed: Folly Island

Dear Mary
  I agane take my pen in hand to wright a fiew lines to you   I have nothing to wright that I know of but the same old story   I am well and eat all before me perfect lazy and begins to dread the the time when I shall have to go to work for a living   if Uncle Sam would let me go home and stay over sunday every week I beleave I would reainlist
  It is warm to day   it is just such a day as it was that day when you and I went out to get beach nuts and John Mass and his wife came up on the hill   And how I wish

we could be under the old beach tree to day or on the hill above but I supose that it is not so nice weather where you are
  We have not had a male cince I wrote before   we expect one Tuesday or Wednesday
Our debate still goes on and the paper is interesting   I got another wipe from the Hospital stuard and agan gave him as good as he sent but I do not supos that you care any thing about my foolery so I will not send you a copy   another week has pased and I have not cut Charles or Danies names   if I am in camp tomorow I will and send them in this leter   I shall

Cup yours and theres in one plate   it will make less weight to send I am making a set of domines that I would like to send home and will if I get a chance   they will be worth about $2,00 if my time was worth any thing and I would rather have them than those that Whitnies boys had   they would please the boyes well   they ar made of segar boxes with a brass face with stars cut throught the brass and the wood is blacked then a rim of britania case round the edge of the wood which holds the brass to its place   I do not think of any thing mor to wright

I was lucky enough to be on gaurd in camp so I have cut your names and spoiled the leter   I and will have to send for a new one   you must practice marking with it   the trouble will be you will use to much ink   ink the brush well on paper or cloth before you tuch

the plates   No more at presant so God bless you all
                    W A Robinson

(stamped on the bottom of this page are block lettered names)

M.E. ROBINSON
C.A. ROBINSON
D.T. ROBINSON

March 20, 1863[45]   This letter was headed: Folly Island, S C

Dear Mary
    I agane sit down to write a fiew lines to you   I am as well as ever and hope this will find you the same   I have recived two leters from you cince I last wrote   the one spoke of Luis being sick and the other that he was beter   I was glad to hear that J Wight had been up as for the money that he should have brought I sent a leter for you and one for Thomas and an acount for him to colect to him by Wm Stott   it apears that he gave him the leter for you but the

what became of the acount I can not tell for it had been all talked over betwen Wight and me before they started that he should colect it when the veterans should get their pay   but it will be all right when they get back as the most is good   the acount was about $15,00   I also gave Stott a brush and botle of ink   it seams that never reached Wight   I will send you a brush but do not know where you can get ink unless I get another chance to send ink   must be thick to mark the plates   Champion might have it or printers ink thined a litle would do

if you cannot get it if you can waite till Sept I will fech ink and use it for you   I have but litle to wright   the time goes so fast with me that it seams like one leter to you all the time   I hardly get the paper put away before I have to get it to wright agane   this makes it rather more pleasant than to have the time drag   there is some prospect of our leaving this Island in the corse of four or five weeks   if we leave it will be for the north eather Newport news Harisburg Pa or New York sity but such good luck is not

---

[45] This letter is dated incorrectly, as it actually was written in 1864

much to be looked for   if we do go we will be Tenesee or Kentucky before our term of servis shall expire   the signes bid fare for us to git out without seeing any more fighting for if we moove it is to join the 9th army corps under Burnside which is to be filed and then act as a resirve cops for the whole army and before it can git in the active servis we will be got out of the servis   no more at presant so good by and God bless and protect you all is the praye of you ever loving husband
William A Robinson

March 25th 1864   This letter is headed: Folly Island

Dear Mary
Another week has roled around and if it is Gods will that we meete agane on earth we are a weeke nearer the time when I last wrote   we are a week near deth any way and may live so as to meat in a hapyer and beter world if not in this   I have nothing new to wright   I am well and hope this will find you the same   I have not had a leter from you cince I last wrote but shall expect one before this starts   we will

for the Vetrans back next Saturday or Sunday and then I shall have that picture that you sent so I might not forget how you looked   this I think heardly posable as I see you to often in my dreams for that   I see you in many a day dreem while ocupied in walking my beat   this is the time I have to think for then I am alone and but litle else to ocupy my atension   it is ther to compose peaces for the Union Star   I send Inclose a statement of W Halsteds efects   keep it with care for with

out doubt I shall be caled on before a cort of justice to sware to it for this is an itim with many others of T L Englands neglect and they can not all go unpunished   I would not stand in his shoes for one thousand dolars if he and som of Co I lives to get home but let this be a secert between you and me for the presant   I have no place to keep such articles here and may send more some time   I shall send some writings home soon that I may want to purblish when I am out of reach of military law and will

expect you to keep them out of sight till that time
27th

The male came yesterde and no leter but like the mans diner it will be the beter when it comes   I am still well and geting fat and the time pases so good by and God bless you all
From your ever loving husband
    W A Robinson
I send the brush in this

Apr 3d 1864   This letter is headed: Folly Island

Dear Mary
    I take this time to wright a fiew lines to inform you that I am well and hope this will find you the same   I recived a leter from you day before yesterday and was glad to hear from you   the veterans came with a male and that money mater that I left with White was all right   he had colected $3,00 and the rest I shall get soone
    I got the likeness last night   I think it a good likness and would like to keep the original to day but I cannot wright to day so good by and may God bless and protect you and the litle ons is the prayer of your ever loving husband
        W A Robinson

Apr 10th 1864   This letter is headed: Folly Island. It is written on white, lined paper.

Dear May
    I take this opertunity of writing a fiew lines to you   I am well and hope this will find you the same   I have not heard from you cince I last wrote   the male came last Friday   I got a leter from Thomas   they was all well in the city   Wesley and Mary was to the City on there way to the west   they too was well   Fannie took the small pox while to the city and caried it hom   I have not heard the result   I shall expect a leter form her the next male which we will git Saturday or Sunday

we will get our pay about Wednes or Thursday of this week   it will be very exceptible though I have plenty of the root of eavil yet about all I use is to by buter   I eat about one pound a week and pay 55 cts per pound   I have got to smoking againe and pay $11,00 per pound for tobaco and use about two pound a month   I supose I smoke about one fourth part my self and treet my friends on the rest but it is all in the family   I have about shook off the homesick spell

96

that I had on when I last wrote and feel a litle more like writing but have not

much to write about   only the same old story which if you ar as tired of hearing as I am writing you would be glad of a litle change I think I would like a small fight just to breake the monotony of camp life but would like a visit home full beter but dont want eather bad enough to rainlist   we have a prayer meeting agoing near camp every night about sundown presided over by a Baptist minister of the Christian Comision   his name is Roundy and he hales from Massichucets   the meetings are good and well atended

this ink is so pail I do not know as you can read this   no more at presant so good by and God bless you all

From your ever loving
husband
    W A Robinson

Apr 17 ' 64 This letter's date began as March, which is crossed out and the Apr written after. It is headed: Folly Island

Dear Mary
  I take this opertunyte of writing a line to you   I am well and hearty and hope this will find you the same   I was sory to hear that mother had lost her horse   I got the leter thursday   We are in a hubbub to day   we are about mooving some where   som think to the North and some think to Floraday   I think North   you will know the next lete   We got our pay to day   I am to busy to wright so good by and God bless you all
    William A Robinson

Apr 25th /64 This letter is headed: Yorktown, Va

Dear Mary
  I met a leter from you at Hilton Head last Wednesday and was glad to hear from you   as I wrote in my last we was on the moove the rigiment started that day which was saturday and Co A and I the provost gaurd started tuesday left Hilton Head Wednesday and arived at Yorktown Sunday yesterday and landed on the side of the york river opisit yorktown   we had as pleasant a voige as ever was maid

or ever will be   I am well as I ever was in my life   I do not know what is to be done with us but

if we ar kept as a provost gaurd I do not care much where we go   I can stand marching if the rest can stand fighting   I was glad to moove to make a change in things and help to pas of the time   last night is the first night I have laid on the ground cince last July   we are agane in hen coop tents and I am siting out dors to write   the wind blows and the sun shine and there is all maner of nois going on around me and if you can read it you can do more than I can   so good by and God bless you all
          W A Robinson

May 1st 1864   This letter is headed: West Point Va

Dear Mary
          I take this opertunity of wrighting a fiew lines to inform you that I am well and hope this will find you the sam   we have not had a mail cinc we left Hilton Head so of corse I have not heard from you   we expect the mail will come up to us soon

We shiped last night from York Town and started this morning for this plase   look on the map and folow the York river to the forks West Point is right at the forks and the tirminous of the railroad that leads to Richond which is about 40 or 50 miles distance   we expect to rebuild a distroyed dock at this place   Co I has returned to the rigiment and Co A is provost gaurd yet under Capt Cormack   I have been detailed to the Pioneer corps which is a good place   I have no gaurd duty or picket to do and have my knapsack caried on a march to make up for this   I have to help put up head quarter tents which takes about 2 hourers   we also have to pull down fences if in the way on a march fix bridges or bad place if nesesary

when in camp we have but litle to do and that litle is work that I like beter than driling or gaurd and the best of all is that we have but litle to do in a fight except in urgent cases   but that makes but litle diferance as long as as the Brigade is comanded by Colonel Alvord of the 3d NYV for he has the gratest slight of keeping out of harms way of any man I ever saw for he has been out over 3 years and his rigiment has neve saw a fight yet and he has wigled us out of several bad scrapes cince he has had comand of the Brigade it is a year the 3d of this month cinc we have had a fight and things look as if it might be some time before we so another though we may be orderd on to Richmond any day but this looks as if Alvord had took time by the fore lock and got the Brigad her to do the work so as to give the rest a chance to do the fighting for if he could fight as well as he can plan to keep out the Rebs would have reason to fear him the boys all say thay hope he will keep in comand till our time is out but I am tired out and will try and finish in the morning

May 2ond
I sent a box from Folly Island directed in the care of Daniel Sackrider Delhi   I wrote to Daniel about it and asked him to send it to Champ or Peters Store   there may be somthing to pay on it   you must find out   there is but litle in the box that you will want   it is my tools and a fiew other things that I could not take on a march   their is som things that I didnot mean to send when I packed it   I calculated to have Wight take it with the Colonels things but an order came out that the oficers could

not take only a certin amount so I took out what I thought of that I wanted and left the rest   there is one pair drawers that ought to come out as soon as you get the box and if you see any thing that you can use take it and leave the rest in the box till I com home   ther is over 50 botle ink   ther is some writing that I may want but nothing special   I put old paper in to fill what I took out   give what domenoes you find to the boyes   there would have been a whole set if I had known ther would have been

a chance to send soon enough but it was tuch and go   there is paper and invelops as much as you will use till I get home   there is some small blocks of lignum vita   save these   there is 3 boxes of mercintile ink that I would rather have lost a dolar than have sent away   they was worth more than that apeace here   I send you $5,00 in this and expect to send the same agane in two or 3 weeks   I have about $50,00 hear but cannot git hold of it yet but it is all good Send me about one tea spoon full of indigo

powder if fine and doo it close in a paper   bluing would be beter if you have it and the first time you get a chance send the same quantity of venitian read and as much yelow ocher   you could get them of Charles Durand but do not put your self out of the way to get them no more at presant so good by and may God bless and protect you all

is the prayer of your ever loving husband
        W A Robinson

May 8 1864   This letter is written in pencil. It is headed: Onward to Richmond Va

Dear Mary
      I take this opertunity of wrighting a fiew line   I am well and feel good   I have not herd from home in a long time   our male has not come up to us yet excep about 25 leter for the whole rigiment and not one of them for Co I so it is no fault of yours but I will wate with patience as long as things ar working well   We have made a small moove since I last wrote   we are now on the south side of the James river and near

Richmond   we landed about one mile above City point   you can find it on the map and have mooved about 8 miles back in the Country   we are some where betwen Petersburgh and Richmond they had a batle to the front yesterday but the storyes are so diferant I hardly know what the result was but he rail road is cut off so the rebs are shut off from each other at the two places   I have nothing to write so I will bid you good by and God bless you all is the prayer of your ever loving husband
        W A Robinson

May 18   This letter is headed: 9 miles from Richmond   It also is written in pencil.

Dear Mary
      I write to inform you that I am well and in good spirits and hope this will find you the same   this is the 3d day we have ben out from camp and do not know how long before we will go back   we have had a litle male but I was not among the lucky ones   We was out monday and tuesday   I was under fire boath dayes and one day cince we was out this time   we are now in the rear doing gaurd duty

the news is all good   we ar doing a fine bussness and whiping the rebs like fun   I wish the back male would come up for I want to hear from home but I know how it is and keep as easy as I can trusting in God that all will be well   the last leter I got was at Hilton Head but I will have pacience   I can do with out male if they will whip the rebs and stop the war   I hope by next saturday to have pen & ink and then I will give you more news but this will be hard to read though I have taken pains to

write plain   no more at presant so good by and God bless you and the Chidren is the prayer of your ever Loving husband
William A Robinson

May 21st 1864 This letter written in pencil is headed: Some Whare

Dear Mary
    I recived two leters from you last night   one Apr 17th and the other Apr 24th and one from Sarah dated Apr 28 to day   I got one from Thomas dated Apr 23d   I do no know where the late male can be but supose it will get along in time   All was well that I heard from except Sarah's man   he was sick in camp and she expected him home soon   there is a grat diferance in her leters since she got maried   she is quiiter like folks

you must excuse pensil writing till I can be in camp long enough to write as we go out with nothing but what we need   I can stick a sheet of paper and an invelop in my cartridge box and write with a pencil but I had no time to write yesterday as we had a spleandid fight we went out on picket night before last and the Rebs comenced picking at us right after dark and we comenced diging rifle pits   this gave the pioneers a chance and we worked by spells for 24 houres only stoping when the bulets flew to thick for

comfort   then we would take our guns get in the ditch and wate for the men in front to be drove in but though the rebs charged on the pickets 12 times they wer repulsed every time and I never got a chance to fire on them   ther was 6 in the 89th wouded and none kiled Thomas Thompson and James Litle in Co I was wonded   I have neve heard such a stidy ratle of musketry in my life   the rebs must have lost severly as they wer not protected by earthworks   other rigiments suferd worse than ours

the 89th got a good deal of creadit for standing there ground aganst a far superior fors and the 39 ohio took a reb general prisonor
I am well and hearty and have not time to get homesick now Thomas has lost his house worth $200   poor felow   he meets with a great deal of bad luck   No more at   presant so good by and God

bless and protect you all   from your ever Loving husband
                    William A Robinson

May 28 1864. This letter is written on very rough paper, described in the letter as captured Rebel paper. It is headed: Near Burmuda Hundred Va

Dear Mary
           I take this opertunity of wrighting a fiew lines to you I am well and hope this will find you the same   I have not recived any leter from you cince I last wrote   I do not know the reason as we get a male every day and I am cirtan there must be be some on the way   I have not had one dated in May while others have them dated the 20th and I have saw one the 24th but I hope it will come out right yet
I took this paper out of a post which when we was distroying the rail road Betwen Richmond & St Petersburgh   it is a good specimin of Rebel wrighting paper and the best they have to do all kinds of business on   so they are not quite indipendent in manufactory yet

We are on the march agane for some plase I know not where but expect to when we get there   we got waked up in the night last Saturday night by musketry which was soon folowed by the noise of canon   two or three shell past over in hearing but the rebs got the worst of the fun   thay had a canon blow up which lit up the sky and made a great cracking which the rebs did not like much   you must not expect long leters when we are on the marsh   so good by and God bless and protect you all is the prayer of your Loving Husband

                    W A Robinson
Send me 8 postage stamps the first chance

Jun 9th 1864 This letter is headed: Dont Know whare

Dear Mary
           I take this opertunity of writing a line to you   I to day recived a leter from you dated May 3d and was glad to hear from you I am sory for Grigory   ther seams to be somthing wrong about the male   I have been som woryed about you but have been to buisy to fret much   I hop the rest of the male will com up soon   some leters comes right through and some dont   I got leter the 2ond from

Wesly dated the 20th they wer well but O how home sick   I hope you get

my leters regular for I see you fel a litle woryed about me but trust in the same God that has keep me safe for depend upon it that he knows best what is for our good Since I wrote last I have had quite a travel   we shiped at City Point and land at White House landing   you can trace the rout on the map down the Jame and up the southern branch of the York   from White House we marched up the railroad tward Richmond   we have been 24 hours in rifle pits and the bulits are flying over head   they has a good many went over since I have been wrighting but I have but litle to do but take care of my self so I am as safe as any whare so dont wory   I expect to be releaved to night and hear that we are to go back eather to Fort Monroe or City Pont   I shall wright every week and if any thing hapens me you will hear of it right away

You wanted to know what I thought of the length of the war   if Lee is taken with Richmond the war is don but if he escapes it may last some time and if we do not suceed

in taking Richmond it will take a year yet but God only knows the result   I feel confident that the 15th of July will see Richmond in our hands and may be the 20th of June and I think that it will be hard for Lee to escape but this is a hard place to wright and the sheet is about fool   I am well and in good spirits and feel as safe as I did on Foly Island   good by and God bless and protect you all and grat that we may meat on earth but may we be priflaged to meat in heaven   from your ever Loving Husband
        W A Robinson

June 11th 1864 This letter is headed: In Rifle pits Va

Dear Mary

    I am right where I was the last time I wrote and in the same state of health   I do not know when we will git out and it makes but litle diferance   I had as live be hear as any where else   the firing is very scarce and goes more so every day   I have recived 3 leters from you the past week   the last was mailed the 1st of June   I think I have recived all up to that tim   they came one a day in order as they wer writen   one had indigo in   I think it a good idea to write more seldom becaus the leters do not com through good and will try it if the male should hapen to bother the other way as of cours you do as you would like to be don by but the Chaplain said in a leter that he wrote home that he had heard more cursing about friends not writing than any one caus and thought more promptness on the part of friends at home would save a great deal of sin in the army so try and wright each week when you can and can get to the ofice I shall alow for delayes knowing how you are situated

I have no news to wright and nothing ilse that I know of so I will make up the lack by growling

I had a leter from Thomas dated the 1st of June all was well in the city he thought I had ought to wright to him several time to his once becaus he was not in as much dange as I but I could not see it in that light it is a great bother to cary pater and fixens to wright and I see mine geting beautifuly small and I must trust to providence to fill up as ther is not a sutler in this place and no one can git out but I shall manage to keep enought to wright each week to you

I can not think of any thing more to wright

so good by and God bless you all and keep you is the prayer of your ever loving Husband
                W A Robinson

June 25th This letter is headed: Near Petersburgh

Dear Mary
      I recived yours of the 16th day before yesterday 17 days is a good while between dates but perhaps ther is one mised I got a leter from Wesley yesterday they wer all well and begin to like it beter there I am well and hopes this will find you the same I have now news to write ther is fighting heare every day but I do not have a hand in I hear the noyes and see the dust fly some times but am quite safe And now about that picture I mean to have a frame on it when I get home and a nice one

if it hapens to cost more than 3 shilings or so tell Hanah if there should be another chance to get them I will get her one tell Jane Ann that if I saw her or James in trouble I would help them if I could or in other words would give them a meal of vitals to save ther lives but when I take trouble to get them a pictur I will take my pay in fresh beef The weather is as hot as a madens first lover and very dry but we loll around in the shade and if we march it is in the night so we get along

very well   I think I shall manage to wory my time out   Wesley advises me not to list agane   he might as well advise me not to shoote my self for I would about as quick do one as the other   I am not sory for what I have done but think I have done my share and am wiling to give my place to som that is crying more blood but have not left home yet   no more at presant so good by and God bless you and the Children is the prayer of your ever loving husband
W A Robinson

July 9th 64 This letter is headed: Near Petersburgh Va

Dear Mary
   I recived a leter form you on the 5th it was writen last month up to 29th and mailed July 1st I think Luis might let you know when he was going to the ofice but it will not be long if God spares my life before you will not be beholden to him   wright as often as you can and I will try and put up with it if some are a good wase apart   the time is giting shorter every day   I do not know what to write   it is the same here one day and samer the next   all the diferance I can see is I washed my shirt yesterday and write a leter today

and tomorow I can stick my fingers in my mouth & waite for it to come night   I hear the roar of canon the crack of rifels & the whiz of ball every day till it hase becom like the roar of a dam to a miler   I do not know that it is going on only noticing it if it stops for a while I want you to tell me how the boys grow and if they talk good and all about that boy of Hanahs and all about the cat and all news in jeneral
   Frank sayes that Sarah is keeping old mades hall and that the last she knew of hew she had bought a bushel of been and she

did not know but she had blew away but I gues she hant as I have had a leter from her cince that   gues this will do for this time   I am well and hearty and hope this will find you the same   you can se that providence has provided me with paper & I think I have enough now to see me throught the cirvis so good by and God bless you all from you ever Loving Husband
W A Robinson

July 16th 1864   This letter is headed: Camp Near Petersburgh Va

Dear Mary
  I take this opertunity of writing a fiew lines to you   I am well and hope this will find you the same   I was hapely disipointed the 10th in reciving a leter from you dated the 6th and mailed the 7th that was quick time and I was not looking for it till the 12th I have saw Domeny Lee of Bovina and Domeny Robinson of Delhi this week and also Ira Twichell of Jefferson   he is in the 3 NY light artilery   the others ar with the Christian Comition

Co I has met with a loss the past week   William Rivenburg was wonded bad with a ball the 12th and Albert W Jones was kiled with a shott from a canon yesterday   the shot pased between Capt Cormack and Lieu Epps head and hurt William Drumonds sholder but not to injure him   it struck Jones in the brest and kiled him in an instant the boyes say they saw his heart beat after it was thrown out   this is an afal day to wright   the wind blows a gale and it takes both hands to hold the paper and the dust files my eyes so I can heardly see you will see

some Virginy soil on the paper and I have to stop between each word to drive the flyes off for they bite like cats
It is three months to day cince we left Folly Island and two Months from to day my time is out acording to the rowls but they are fals and I expect nothing but ther will be a fus about it and if there is I may be kept till the 21st of October so you must not be to sure of my coming home   the mater will be setled by the 16th of next month and I will let you know the result as sone as I find out my self

but there is one thing cirtain   I can get pay and cloths from the 16th of sept and they can not get that back
I think I shall put off writing till a stiller day so good by and god bless and protect you all is the prayer of your ever Loving husband
    W A Robinson

July 24th/64   This letter is headed: Near Petersburgh Va

Dear Mary
  I recived a leter from you the night that I wrote last and sent you a book the next day in answer to it   I wrote a word in the back side   I intended to inclose a leter   from Sarah but it wold show

so as to spoil the chance   I inclose it in this   I am well and hearty and hope this will find you the same   I have no money but they are paying the troops and we expect ours every day   I will send as soon as I can most likly you will get money in the next letter   I want you to get all

you can of mother with out puting her to trouble as I want all the money I can rase when I get home   If you see any of Aunt Rhody folks let her know that I shall want all I can get but shall not hury her till the first of January   I will wait on mother till the first of Jan for all that she can not pay before but from now till I get home   I do not want to pay her any money till I get home unless she needs it bad there is between $75 & $100, due me hear now and at my final setlement I shall get about $150, so I will have something to do with once in my life if

God see fit to spare me and I intend to try to do somthing   We are two dayes in camp and two dayes in the rifle pits   we came out of the pits last night is the reason that I did not write yesterday and next time the rigiment goes out it is my turn to stay in camp so I get six days in camp this time
You wanted to know what I was doing   I am not with the Co   I wrote you 2 month ago I am in the pianear corps a detail from each Co making 10 men comanded by a sargent to do the head quarter work which averages about an hourer per day and we get rid of the nasty part of fighting   I

was a mile off on the 16th 17th and 18th of June while the boys was fighting but I have to go when the rigiment goes on picket but do not have to stand gaurd except on extream ocasions   I have not stood gaurd but twice cince I left Folly Island   We are incamped in a small corn field   I have saw a part of it biger than Jims and mothers farm put to gather and there is one side that I have not seen as the rebl rifle pits go through it which make the climate on that side rather unhealthy   our camp is a mile from the rebel pits and the field goes nearly a mile back of us and I do not know how far back of the rebs Good by and God bless you all from your ever loving husband
                              W A Robinson

July 31st 1864   This letter is headed: Camp Near Petersburgh   Each page is written on stationary with the printed heading U. S. Sanitary Commission.

Dear Mary

I recived a leter from you last sunday night and another of the 24th to 26 to night   I have waited til the male came in hopes that I might hear from you and was not disapointed   I should have writen yesterday but the 89th had an invitation to atend a ball at the ground ocupied by the 9th Army corps yesterday morning and as I supose you would like to hear the particulars I will give them to you   we wer orderd to pack and be ready at a moments notice about 5 oclock

friday night and recived orders about 11 to go in light marching order and start at once   it was about 2 miles and took till about 3 before we wer mased and ready for a dance but the music was not yet ready so we lay down and took an american nap with about as much harness on as a horse the ground for a bed the sky for a cove and a canteen for a pilow and lay there till dawn when we wer awaked by the musick for the first set   We had heard that the 9th corps was mining 2 of the Johneys forts and the musick comenced by

leting them both off at a time and some of the rebs waked to find they had taken themselves wings and was already from 30 to 50 feet in the air with guns and gun cariges aminiton and other inplyments of war folowing after and at the same time we opned on them with a large nomber of canon and charged ther works   the 89th with the rest from the 18th and 10th Army corps was held in reserve and the 9th did the work   There is a great many conflicting reports about the batle and you will probably hear the results about as soon as I shall   I am well and hope this may find you

injoying the same blessing   Daniel Mains of Co I was slightly wondens in the sholder to day in the pits   as soon as they returned I did not have to go so I got 10 dayes in camp this time with the exception of atending the ball   As for pay I expect it soon and have for some time   there is four months due up to the first of July   this is all we will if paid before the 10 of Sept then we would get 6 month pay   the first 2 months due me is $14 per month and I do not know

what I am giting now but $16 any way and I expect $18 as I expect the pay of a corporal of cavelry which is $18 the same as infantry now but was one dolar more under the old law but it may be that the wagnor dose not get any more than a private now   The vetrans are expecting ther state bounty every day now and when they come ther is money enough due me that I can send you what you want and I will send it as soon at it comes

My prospect for giting discharged befor the 21st of october looks rather dim at presant   I think the

government is rather hard on the old 3 years men and will loose by it for they now what belongs to them an will kick if there rights ar infringed on   keeping them will tell a tail at election   I have no more to wright so good by and God bless and protect you is the prayer of your ever Loving Husband
          William A Robinson

August 7th 1864   This letter is headed: Camp Near Petersburgh Va

Dear Mary

    I just recived yours last tuesday and was glad to hear from you I recived one from Frank last night and answered it day   I am under the weather to day and excused from duty   it is the 3d day cince the first of Dec   yesterday I did a hard dayes work and feel as if I should be beter tomorow   the rigiment goes to the pits to night but I shall not go

We have no pay yet but expect it every day and when it comes I will send you what money you want

you nead not make excuses for using money for if I thought you used more than you neaded I should not send it to you   but I wish to know what to look for   I know that things are high but do not know how high and expect you will make yourself and children comfortable as long as the money can be got

If Mother talks of seling out I will buy her out if she can not do any beter than I will do by her but do not wish to except I can give satisfaction   there is no hopes of my giting home till the 21st of October but that will

role around in time so we must have patience   I manage to get all the money I wish to spend by washing fore the boyes and trust some beside that can not raise money but the most keep giting a litle from home so they can pay such things   I have a good deal out but it will come around right soon   I think we will get pay before the week is out as part of our brigade is paid all ready but pay goes slowe on acount of money being scarce with the pay master   but the day it comes you shall have som and if you   could borow som it will be safe to promis to

pay soon   I have no news to write and will bid you a good by and God bless and protect you and the Children is the prayer of your ever loving husband
>> William A Robinson

August 18th 1864 This letter is headed: Camp Near Peterburgh Va

Dear Mary
>> As I have the good luck to have $2,00 to spare I thought to write a fiew lines and send it along   this leter must answer for this week so you must not look for an other in about 10 dayes and then you can look for more mony as I am making a litle along now washing   could make more if money was pleanty in the rigiment the most money I get comes from rigiments that have had ther pay we hear the pay master is coming and so is

chrismas and I gues they will get hear about to gather but I have had all the money that I could aford to spend but maid it as I went along and now I have a litle to spare   I am well but have a sore leg that keeps me in camp and with a litle nursing will keep me from going to the pits for some time

I saw the greatest sight last monday that I ever saw of the kind   the camp of the 18th army corps is along a revine and a stream runs through it about as large as the one that runs from your hous down to Jims   it comenced to rain in the after noon

and in les than an hower the stream was so high that it caried off intire rigiments tents and shades that had been put up with logs barels boxes and every thing moovable came rushing dow the stream with the speed of a rase horse   the camp of the 89th was about half washed away and a good many of the boys ar out a knapsack and all the cloths they had excep what they had on   Co I was among the sufferors   I lost nothing except a peace of skin off my shin and I mean to get pay for that by giting rid of duty about a month if it does not heel up to quick

there was also a good many lives lost   ther was 22 dead taken out of the brook that night and I heard ther was over 40 lost all to gather the 55th Penn suferd the worst   they lay next to the 89th and up the stream   several sutlers was washed   away   one lost all he had even to his trunk with eleven thousand dolars in   I have got up I dont know how many times cince I began this but one time I maid a dolar clear and will add it to the 2 for you   we mooved camp about a mile and a half yesterday and are very buisy to day fixing up

I wish you would subscribe for that magisenee if you can   I would send from hear but have forgot the adress   I will send you 2 or 3 dolars more the next time I write and if we get pay will right the day it comes if tomorow   I send a paper this week for the boyes   read it and then let them have the picturs to ply with and tell them to be good boys and papa will com home soon and fech them some thing nice tell Dan and Luis that if they are caled out it will be only 100 dayes and in the defences of Washington at that

so they need not get scared yet but if the draft of the 5 of next month caches them they will have a year in the army of the Potomack wich is soldering in earnest   I have no more to write at presant so good by and God bless and protect you is the prayer of your ever Loving husband
                W A Robinson

P S if you can read this you can beet me

August 26th 64 This letter is headed: Camp at Point of Rocks Va

Dear Mary
        I now sit down to write a fiew lines to you   I recived yours of the 14th last monday and was glad to hear from you   We mooved camp agane yesterday   mooved about 5 or 6 miles and crosed the Appamatox river at point of rocks and camped near there in a good camp   we fixed up quite nice now and look like live thou perhaps you would think we had poor houses   the worst is we are so loansom we do not know what to do   we cant sleep for we

miss the crack crack of muskets and the whiz whiz of ball which we have not been out of hearing of befor in so long that it seams strange and the last camp we was in shells used to visit us as often as was pleasant   one burst in a mans bed about 10 minutes after he had got out the first night we was ther and filed my tent so full of smoke that I had to dig out   the next night a peace of shell went through my tent but we are well off from the rebs hear   if we can be let aloan hear it is all right   we was orderd hear for   a rest my health is good at presant   my leg is giting beter   I walked on it yesterday   it maid it prity sore and painful but the prospect is that I can not make it last over a week longer   it is two weeks monday since it was hurt   I had a leter from Thomas two dayes ago   he is ofall fraid of the draft and comes down on old Abe at a great rait   I would send you the leter but there is some directions in it that I may want in about 2 months if God spares my life till then   you shall have the next leter I get from Mary   I might

have sent them before but did not think of it and leter does not last long with me unless ther is somthing in that I wish to keep as I can not cary them around   no more at presant so good by and God bless you and the children is the prayer of your ever Loving husband
W A Robinson

Sept 1st 1864   This letter is headed: Camp Near Point of Rocks Va

Dear Mary
I recived yours of the 25th two dayes ago and one from Frank and Sarah at the same time   Sarah had been sick but boath was well at the time of writin   Frank spoke of geting a leter from you   I am well at presant   comenced doing duty on my leg monday but have but litle to do   we are as safe hear as a thief in the mill   neve hear any thing that sounds ugly and I sincerely hope they will let us bee hear the rest of our time

No pay yet and prospects not as good as they wer for giting any soon we was musterd yesterday for sixmonth pay & I expect mine is an eaven hundred   I think a hundred dolar bill will look good to me when it comes and the boyes owe me enough to keep you and me the rest of my time out   I looked in my pocketbook when I red your leter and found just 25 cts and thought I could not spair that so I went around the rigiment and gathered up a pair of waches and took to a rigiment that had been paid   result $5,00 in which I send you

and will try and do so agane by the time I will write agane as we will not git pay till after the 10 of the month now   I shall put the last stamp on this agane   so I dont wory my tim keeps waring away and the time will soon come when I shall be with you God willing   I have no news so good by and God bless you all is the prayer of your ever loving husband

William A Robinson

Sept 8 th 1864 This letter is headed: Fort Powhatan Va

Dear Mary

The mail has just come and no leter from you and I must wait another day and was a good mind to make you waite too   we mooved day befor yesterday and have got fixed up nice   we are about 20 miles below city Point on the James river and quite out of the way of the rebes but we got weaned of them a little while at the Point of Rocks   it was a good idea to move us a litle way at a time as we could

not have slept nights if the musick had all stoped at a time   I am well and hope this will find you the same   I sent you $5,00 in this and want to know if it is good   I can get it at a discount hear that will pay if it pases good where you are   I sent an Iowa bill to Wesley   it was $200   I got it for 25 cts and told him if it was not good to give it to the children to play with   there is a man hear with a $50,00 bill that I shall take if the pay was to ever get around which is

doubtful in the extram   I think we will just put hear   I think we will stay hear and be discharged and filed up   there is about 130 to be discharged this fall   part of them their time is out now and expect to be mustered out every day but the moove and other causes is keeping them which makes them mad and I would be if I was in their place   oficers that must look out for their coats when we get home or they will git on them   I have no news to write so

good by and God bless and protect you all is the prayer of you ever loving husband
　　　W A Robinson

My hand swet so this looks as if quail had tracked it but you nead not looke for another till I hear from you
　　　　　W A R
I sent you $5,00 in the last I wrote   let me know how much you have recived   I sent you $3,00 once before making with this #13,00

Sep 16th 1864 This letter is headed: Fort Powhattan Va

Dear Mary
       I am mad to write but thought to say a word   I am well and hope this will find you the same   I had a pas yesterdy to got to City Point   had a nice ride on boat 20 miles and back   neve was 3 miles away from the rigiment before
   Well I am a Conscript now as my time is out   would like to see roten eggs droping off old Fairchilds coat and perhaps will about the 21st of next month   I had a litle more money I went to send

but buisness interfeard so I could not send it in two dayes yet and thought you would rather waite for the money than a leter   no more at presant so good by and God bless and protect you all is the prayer of your ever Loving husbad
       W A Robinson

Sept 24th 1864   This letter is headed: Fort Powhattan Va   It is written on lined stationary with a U.S. Sanitary Commission heading.

Dear Mary
       In my last I forgot to mension the recipet of a leter the sunday before which was 2 weeks ago to day and I recived one last night telling of the inlist-ments of Dan and Luis   they got good bounties but I could do beter than that if I wished to stay   I have been oferd $100, per month to go in a sutler store but home is what I want and will tend to making mony after I get there

We got our pay this morning   I get an even hundred   I get $18, per month since the first of may so I got $10, more than the privates this time and $2, more than corporals   you wanted to know just when I would be home   that is just what I want to know   I expect to start the 21st of Oct but Co Bs time was out the 3d and its the 5 and Fs the 9th of this month and there has not a man been let to go but the talk is that all will be kept

till the 21st and all be discharged togather   Co I and K was sworn in that day and was the last Co
there is a breeze a raising and will blow stiff soon if ther is not discharging done and the grand king of the 89th had beter look wild for breakers when we all get in sivil life and stand on evan ground you spok as if you had recived that state bill though you only have mensioned the 3 & one 5   I have   sent one 5 green back   I

send 3 in states mony now   I shall not send
any more till I come ore find out that I have to stay for life   if you
nead money borow if you can for you shall have it to pay by the 5th
day of Nov if express me does not fail   but there is no doubt but I
will be there by that tim and likly 10 dayes befor   I am well and
hope this will find you the sam   Good by and God bless and protect
you all is the prayer of your ever Loving husband
W A Robinson

Oct 6th 1864 This letter is headed: Near Point of rocks VA

Dear Mary
        I take this opertunity of writing a fiew lines to you   I am
where I was the last leter I wrote to you and the regiment is still
somewhere near Richmand   we do not know whether the regiment
will com here or we be sent ther yet and I care but litle as the fighting
is don for the presant   Dan Lee was taken prisnor   As for my health
is is good   I am giting ove the bad spell that I had when I last wrote
and can get around comfortable but would no be able to

fight if there should be any more   Co C was musterd out this morning
and a happy lot of felows they wer   they will leave her at 9 oclock
tomorrow   they are having a high old tim here to day   Co I will be
musterd out on the 21st and start the 22ond so two weeks from
tomorrow I shall be a free man agane   we will get to Fort Monroe at
night but will have to stay ther one day to setle up and get pay   we
will leave ther the 24th and arive in NY the night of the 25th I shall
stay ther two dayes and leave ther the night of the 27th and get hom

the night of the 28 about 9 or 10 oclock at night as I shall have to
walk from Delhi   now this is calculating for no acodent and meeting
trains and all compleat so I may not get home so quick by two dayes
as I expect to so don't wory till the 1st day of Nov   I shall write agane
about a week from to day and tell you how I get along and that will
finish up my writing   I have not heard from you in almost two weeks
I hope to get a leter soon and will not have to look in van for but one
more leter from you   so good by and

God bless you alll is the prayer of your eve loving husbany
W A Robinson

Oct 13th 1864. This is the final letter written by soldier, soon to be civilian again, William A. Robinson to his wife Mary. It is headed: Camp Near Point of Rock

Dear Mary

I now sit down to adress you for the last time God willing till I shall see you a week from tomorrow   I shall be a free man but Oh how long it seems and how slow the time goes   it seam an age cince we left Powhataan and it is only two weeks   I recived yours of the 25th & 28 befor yesterday and one from Thomas the same day dates the 1st   he was well and in a great hury for my time to be out so I could get there to see

him   my visit ther will be short as I must go ove to Brooklyn to see Lucy and I have some buisness to do in NY and two dayes is all I will spare for the whole for it seems as if I should fly till I can get home tell Charly that Pa will soon be home now and tell Danie that I dont beleave his feet is big enough to fit boots but if they are and he is a good boy he shall have them   I shall be home Friday the 28 if every thing works right but a miss in any plase will keep me till Saturday and some of the boys have

had to stay two dayes at fort Munroe and as ther is about 30 of us to start in one day our chance is slim for gitin off short of two dayes but depend upon it I shall be ther as quick as I can get ther   I am well and hearty   am about 10 miles from the rigiment doing guard duty over a lot of camp equipage and like to stay the rest of my tim so let them fight they wont hit me   the wind blows so that I do not know as you can read this   if you can you can beat me   I do not think of any

more to write so good by and may God in his mercy wach over all and grant that we may meat as soon as we expect to is the prayer of your ever loving husband
                    W A Robinson

Chapter Four
Eighty Ninth New York Volunteer Infantry Regiment

Organization and Enlistment

Despite the optimistic views of the majority of the populace at the time, that is that the war would be over in short order, President Lincoln in July of 1861 saw the need for longer term volunteers for the Union Army. Prior to that time, most volunteers were enlisting for three-month terms of service. That July, President Lincoln requested from Governor Morgan of New York, who in his turn on July 25th called for 25,000 New York men to enlist for three-year terms. By August, various depots were established around New York to raise the necessary units.

The Honorable Daniel S. Dickinson, the former Senator from the State of New York, received authority on August 29th, 1861 to raise a regiment of infantry. This Regiment was organized under Col. Harrison Stiles Fairchild. The Regiment was raised in central New York, from Broome, Chenango, Delaware, Livingston, Monroe, and Schuyler counties. The companies were recruited essentially as follows: A, at Havana; B and H at Binghamton; C, at Mount Morris; D, at Rochester; E, at Norwich and Oxford; F, at Whitney Point; G, at Windsor; I, at Delhi; and K, at Corbettsville. With patriotic fervor, the various companies gathered together near their homes, and had inspiring send-offs. The experience of the men called the Delaware Rifles, later to become Company I, may have been typical. In October, the company was drawn up in front of Hunter's Hotel in Delhi. There were addresses by the Honorable S. Gordon and the Honorable C. Hathaway, followed by "an impressive prayer" by the Reverend Eggleston. Following this, the men marched through the village escorted by the Fire Department, the Delaware Battery (another unit forming at the time) and no doubt many cheering folks along the festive way.

The 89th formally joined together at Elmira late in November, where they lived in barracks and where they were mustered into the service of the United States on Dec. 4th, 5th, and 6th of 1861.

The regimental officers at mustering-in were:

Colonel: Harrison S. Fairchild
Lieut. Col.: Jacob B. Robie
Major: Daniel T. Everts
Adjutant: John E. Shepard
Quartermaster: Cornelius H. Webster
Surgeon: Truman H. Squire
Assistant Surgeon: William A. Smith
Chaplain: Nathaniel E. Pierson

The 89th, now formed and mustered, left promptly for Washington on Dec. 6, 1861. They became known as the Dickinson Guard. Company I, which had been raised in Delhi, initially called itself the Delaware Rifles. They traveled through Pennsylvania on two separate trains. One train was involved in an accident, but apparently without significant injury. Arriving in the vicinity of the Washington outskirts, the 89th was assigned to the Army of the Potomac in the defense of Washington. Those early days were spent establishing their camp, drilling in military fashion, and getting familiar with their weapons. They were issued muskets, not the hoped-for rifles. Most of the men had the opportunity to visit the nation's capital and many had photographs taken to send to loved ones. Disease, boredom and homesickness, not war, were the problems the men faced at this juncture. The men were anxious to have news of the war and even more so to have news from home. Overly optimistic predictions of the imminent collapse of the Southern cause were rampant. Mail call and mustering for pay were the most longed-for events, and the only other thing coming close was hoping for or dreaming about a furlough. For the 89th, the first camp out of New York, which they called Camp Clay, was not to be home for long. They were soon to leave for further south. Before leaving however, Senator Dickinson presented the Regiment with its Colors on the last day of 1861.

1862

The 89th was assigned in January, 1862 to Burnside's Expedition to North Carolina. They traveled by transport from Virginia into the Atlantic to North Carolina. The journey took many of the New Yorkers on their first ocean voyage. They were nearly four weeks aboard the ship Aracan, including time lying in harbor. They first were encamped near Hattaras Inlet, but late in February were ordered to move to Roanoke Island. There they established a rather comfortable camp that they called Camp Dickinson.

The Eighty Ninth at the Battle of South Mills/Camden, North Carolina
(for correlation see letters dated April 8th, 21st and particularly the 22nd, 1862)

One of the objectives of the Burnside Expedition was to threaten Norfolk, VA by way of the southern approach. Accordingly on the 17th and 18th of April, 1862, the third division with Brigadier General Reno commanding, embarked on transports from Roanoke Island bound for the Pasquotank on the north of the Albermarle Sound, and debarked a little south of Elizabeth City. The object of this move was to destroy locks that allowed the movement of Confederate gunboats from Norfolk across the Dismal Swamp to Albemarle Sound. The 89th was part of the fourth Brigade, commanded by Col. Rush Hawkins, the colonel of the 9th NY. This brigade included the 9th and 89th NY, and the 6th NH regiments. The strength of the 89th was recorded as 650 men in the reports. The fourth brigade was the first to land, the other two regiments' transports having gotten delayed by about four hours at the mouth of the river. Col. Hawkin's brigade left at about 3 AM for their objective, a bridge at South Mills, that they were to take and hold. They however, whether due to darkness, poor guidance or bad judgement, marched some ten miles out of the way, and were passed by the later arriving, but fresher troops, which included the 21st MA and 51st PA regiments along with a small artillery unit. Col. Hawkin's men were ordered to follow. The heat and dust were now said to be oppressive, and many men were exhausted by the time they reached enemy positions some four miles further. Most of the regiments had large numbers of stragglers. General Reno was just about to order a halt for rest and a meal, the men having not eaten formally all day, while marching since dawn (or before), when the body came under fire. The advance guard had failed to see the concealed and entrenched rebel forces.

Under fire from Confederate artillery, Gen. Reno immediately began an advance, and it was then mid-afternoon. The 51st PA was ordered to the right to try to flank the defenders, advancing through a wooded approach with its barberry underbrush, and with the 21st MA following. They engaged the rebel left line after meeting and pushing the skirmishers back, and gradually they weakened it. The 6th NH remained to the left of the approaching road, with the small artillery unit, and continued to harass the enemy right, while slowly advancing. The 9th NY and 89th NY were ordered to follow the path of the 51st and 21st in support. For reasons that are not clear, Col. Hawkins ordered his regiment, the 9th NY, to charge across the open field with the 89th in support and following, instead of making way in the woods, as General Reno insisted he ordered. The 9th reached about 200 yards from the entrenched rebels, where they were met by an explosive artillery barrage of grape and cannister with a destructive musket volley, which halted the charge. They then moved slowly right towards the woods, some joining the 51st, and now the 89th was in the lead and continued to advance. The effect of the (probably unauthorized) charge on the defending rebels, though, did allow the 51st and 21st to over-run the enemy's left flank and the confederates retreated, leaving their works and some artillery. In the final attack of the 51st and 21st, the defiant color-sergeant of the rebel defending regiment was shot.

The time was then approaching dark. While some officers wished to pursue the retreating rebels, others felt they had insufficient ammunition for another battle, and most felt that the men were exhausted. In the end, the men laid on the field of battle resting with their arms until ordered to withdraw at about 10 PM. The march back to the boat landing was most arduous due to showers that turned the road to mud, said to be from three to fifteen inches thick. On return to their boats just before dawn of the 20th, the men had marched 35 (the fourth brigade had marched about 45) miles in heat and then mud, and had fought a heated battle with little nourishment the whole time, all in the course of about 24 hours.

The confederate reports indicated a defense with about 600 infantry composed of the 3rd Georgia and a North Carolina militia, along with a company of cavalry and four artillery pieces. The union estimate was of about 1800 defenders. Colonel Wright, the Confederate commander of the battle estimated the attacking strength at about 5000 men. The truth is that the numbers of combatants that day had no overwhelming superiority of numbers or materiel on either side. Both sides claimed the battle as a victory. The union position was that the rebels retreated from their defensive positions, and suffered heavily. They claimed Norfolk would have been frightened by the defeat. The Confederate position was that the Yankees failed to pursue their withdrawal, and left the region the next day in their boats, leaving behind powder and wounded, surely indicating they were the defeated. The locks were not destroyed.

In the aggregate, Union army reports state there was one union officer killed and nine wounded, and 12 enlisted men were killed while ninety-two were wounded. There were thirteen enlisted men listed as missing. There were no deaths in the action from the 89th, but there were four men wounded (possibly Lt. William Cahill of Co. A, Cpl. Averill Harris of Co. A, and Pvts. Benjamin Craft of Co. C with Patrick Sullivan of Co. A) and two (possibly Sgts. Michael Buckley and Sidney Gwynne, both of Co. D) listed as missing. Some twenty or so Federal wounded were left behind with an assistant regimental surgeon, and most were later paroled. Confederate army reports of their casualties are not clear, although the captain in command of the artillery unit was killed. An aggregate Confederate casualty number of about 70 killed, wounded and missing was given in a report to General Robert E. Lee. Regardless of the views of outside observers and historians, the men of the 89th who took part in the battle felt they had been part of a victory. They arrived without further incident back on Roanoke Island a bedraggled, weary lot of men.

The 89th remained at Camp Dickinson until July 10th when they left for Norfolk, Virginia, arriving on the 12th. This was after McClellan's failed 1862 Peninsular Campaign, and the Union armies were left consolidating their strongholds near the coast. By mid August they were on the move again. Burnside's corps was moved to northern Virginia to join with Pope's Army stationed at the Rapidan River. The central leadership in Washington was calling for McClellan's Army on the Peninsula to return, and Lee was not waiting for the combination to be completed. His army, purposely divided, came behind Pope's forces, forcing Pope to move north, taking the pressure off from Richmond, and then defeated Pope's army at Bull Run. McClellan was slowly getting his forces north, but again Lee was on the move.

The Maryland Campaign
(For correlation see Letters dated September 24, and 28, 1862)

The 89th, still part of the Ninth Corps moved to northern Virginia, and encamped near Fredericksburgh. They were on detached duty guarding bridges, and were not fighting at Bull Run, General Pope's great defeat. Unknown to them though, they were approaching the times of their most severe fighting. Lee was planning his first major invasion of the North. Lee's army crossed the Potomac into Maryland early in September, writing to President Davis that he would take the war to the north, and was secretly hoping that the decisive battle against McClellan could be fought in the north. Lee's army moved north behind the screen of South Mountain. His plan was calculated against heavy numerical odds, but he counted on the habitual sloth of McClellan and the great faith he had in his soldiers. Readers may remember that in that early September of 1862, as Lee's army left Frederick, Maryland, one of his officers lost the written orders, found later by the Union army, and this was in the hands of General McClellan by September 13. General McClellan moved to meet the invasion, no longer a secret.

The 89th was among the units at the Battle of South Mountain/Boonesborough, where the armies clashed in Maryland. All combatants had been marching long and hard the days prior to, and for many also including that Sunday of battle. Detailed in the Third Division, under General Rodman, in the First Brigade led by Col. Fairchild, the 89th was then under the temporary command of Major Jardine. The regiment was intended to be a support unit, but while they were arrayed protecting a battery, Battery E of the Fourth Artillery probably led by Captain Clark, they were surprised and attacked by elements of four North Carolina Regiments. These, portions of the North Carolina 2nd, 4th, 12th, and 13th (according to Confederate records, while the Union records report them as North Carolina 2nd, 3rd, 13th, and 30th) were under the command of Brigade General Anderson, a part of the division of Major General D.H. Hill, of Longstreet's Corps. They attacked through a cornfield, yelling as they charged. The rebel aim was the capture of the battery, hoping in so doing to flank the extreme left of the Union lines at South Mountain. In this defense, the 89th had the major role. The other regiments of the brigade were already in line of battle and trudging up the slope further ahead. The 89th repelled the attack, saved the battery, and possibly the left of the whole line. When the battery was secure, they were moved further up the mountain in support of the attacking brigade. Fighting continued until darkness set in, although the further action of the 89th was very limited. They had 3 killed (privates Christopher Knight of Co. K; and Levia Moore and Uri Morse both of Co. G) and 18 wounded (including Lewis Heath, a sergeant of Co. G; and private Edward Porter of Co. G, who died thirty one days later in hospital) that September 14th, 1862. They also captured 30 prisoners. The Confederates withdrew during the night after the battle at South Mountain. General Lee reported hearing that Crampton's Pass had also been taken, and with his army divided in enemy territory, he felt it would be better to concentrate his forces together at Sharpsburg. On the morning of the 15th, the Union army awoke to the news that the Confederates had indeed left, and considered their actions the day before as part of a great victory. But the invaders were not destroyed, and on the same day it was confirmed that Harper's Ferry had surrendered to the rebels. Union cavalry fanned out looking for the Confederates, and soon discovered their route.

On the afternoon of the September 15th, the ninth corps left the vicinity moving in pursuit and by the 16th was encamped on the east shore of the Antietam Creek, near Sharpsburgh. On the 16th, the Union forces held a significant numerical superiority, but the cautious McClellan took the day to study the situation. McClellan finally attacked the well-entrenched confederate positions on the 17th. This battle, called Antietam or Sharpsburg, has the painful distinction of having resulted in more American soldiers killed and wounded in one day of battle than there ever had before or since occurred. The 89th was still in the Ninth Corps under Burnside. This corps was on the extreme left line of the Union array again on that day. Their objective was to cross the stone bridge, and then to take the heights beyond. Another portion of the command, which was to include the 89th, was detailed to ford the Antietam Creek further to the left to aid in the assault on the heights. If accomplished, this would permit flanking fire on the right of Longstreet's central forces. The bridge was defended by two veteran Georgia Regiments, the 2nd and 20th, along with a small battery on the heights above commanded by Captain Eubank. All of these were under General Robert Toombs, leading a brigade of General David R. Jones' Division of Longstreet's Corps. Successive assaults on the stone bridge first by the 11th Conn., then by the 6th NH and 2nd Maryland regiments were each repulsed by the Georgians with heavy Union loss. Finally the 51st NY and 51st PA regiments succeeded in crossing the bridge at about 1 PM, and were rapidly followed by the remainder of the division. Meanwhile General Rodman's Division including the 89th, managed to cross the ford further along. This section was poorly defended by the depleted 50th Georgia Regiment. Lacking sufficient guns and failing to have any reinforcements to defend, all of the Georgia Regiments of the Confederate right line were withdrawn by General Toombs to the heights. Partway up the slope was a stone wall, carefully defended, and the whole slope was partly wooded, providing ample cover for the rebel defenders. The whole of this part of the Union force attacked and drove the confederate forces before them, capturing the heights, several batteries including McIntosh's Battery, and elements even moved into the town of Sharpsburgh beyond. At about that time, detached units of General Toombs own brigade (the 17th and remainder of the 50th Georgia Regiments) arrived, and as is more often represented in history, the division of General A.P. Hill arrived on the field, having just marched from Harper's Ferry. They immediately shelled and attacked the left flank of the Union forces just after the Union success in the capture of the high ground. The Union forces were ordered by General Burnside to withdraw, although the Confederate report language says the Union forces fled in disarray back to and across the stone bridge. Undoubtedly there are elements of truth in both sides' reports, but whichever is the most accurate, the ground so painfully gained by the Ninth Corps was lost very quickly, all except the bridge which remained under Union control. In the earlier assault, Private Thomas Hare of Company D of the 89th captured the colors of some South Carolina Regiment, which was later presented to General Burnside. Pvt. Hare was killed a short while later. Darkness brought an effective end to the conflict of September 17th, 1862. The 89th had total losses of 19 killed (which included Cpl. William Beers of Co. C; Pvts. Solomon Brown of Co. C, Charles Courtney of Co. G, George Eaglesfield of Co. K, Daniel Edson of Co. G, George English of Co. F, Nathaniel Forrest of Co. A, and Henry Francisco of Co. A; Cpl. Lyman Mills of Co. K; Sgt. Adam Needick of Co. B; Cpl. John Pixley of Co. A; Sgt. Nicholas Rulapaugh of Co. C; Pvts. Stephen Scovel of Co. H, George Sherwood of Co. F, Adelbert VanAntwerp of Co. C, and Samuel Wasson of Co. A; Sgt. William Wick of Co. A; Pvt. Lanora Wilson of Co. C; and possibly Linus Morse of Co. H); 77 wounded (which included Pvts. Joseph Andrews of Co. F, Franklin Bacon of Co. H, and Andrew Bartholomew of Co. F who died from his wounds about two months later; Sgt Charles Booth of Co. F who had to be discharged in the January following; Pvt. Thomas Brown of Co. G; Cpl. Jehiel Cameron of Co. B; Pvt. Milton Cresson of Co. G who was also captured but paroled about six months later; Pvts. Dewitt Gilbert, Philip Grodwant of Co. G, James Holden of Co. A, and Willis Humfrey of Co. C; Sgt. William Perkins who later returned to Co. G and was wounded again in 1864; Cpls. Thomas Piersall and Franklin Plunkett of Co. G; Pvt. Almon Reed of Co. F; Pvts. Milton Tompkins and Samuel Twitchell both of Co. G; Lt. Garrett VanIngen of Co. F; and probably Richard Gray who died September 22nd 1862 from wounds); and 8 missing (including Pvts. Martin Dewey and Joseph Swagart both of Co. G) at the Battle of Antietam. Some of those listed as missing probably deserted.

The following day, McClellan failed to press, Lee retreated that very night, and the Maryland campaign was essentially over. The 89th stayed in the vicinity, and camped near Harper's Ferry, Maryland, recovered when the rebels retreated back to Virginia. On November 5th, General Burnside replaced General McClellan, and the members of the 89th, which had now been under the command of Burnside since January, found themselves moving with his Army of the Potomac into northern Virginia.

Fredericksburgh Campaign
(for correlation see letters of November 19, December 2, 7, 18, and 28 of 1862, and those of January 11, 19 and 25 of 1863)

When Gen. Burnside took command, it was McClellan's army to most of the men. An exception might have been to the Ninth Corps, but Burnside took time to arrange his command and his plan. The officials back in Washington expected him to lead his army across the Rappahanock River northwest of Fredericksburg, Virginia, and then to move along its south bank. Burnside determined that it could not be done by fording, and instead requested enough pontoons to create bridges to cross the river, to be supported by gunboats. His plan was to do this at Fredericksburg. However, he did not leave with his main body from Warrenton until November 15th. By November 21st, when General Sumner's portion of the army including the 89th was near Falmouth, there was only a small Confederate force holding the city of Fredericksburg just to the south. But, the pontoons did not arrive until November 25th, the gunboats could not move that far upstream, and by this time the movement of the army and movement of the pontoons was known to Lee, and he was hastening to counter. When Burnside noted the concentration of the forces, he determined that a new plan was needed, this one to include a crossing in the face of opposition. Unfortunately for the Union troops massing on the north side of the river, this created further delay until the 10th of December. Morale in the camps of the Union soldiers was low. Public opinion back home was many times against further fighting, the weather was getting cold and the camps uncomfortable, and many soldiers had not been paid in months. Desertions, which were always an issue for the army, started to increase. This increased rate also was seen in the 89th NYVI, when men such as James Cassidy, Pvt. of Co. H, Sherman Cook, Pvt. of Co. B; Henry and Moses Davis, Pvts. of Co. H; Stephen Galloway, Pvt. of Co. K; William McConnell, Pvt. of Co. D; Russell Perry, Pvt. of Co. K; and Henry Wilson, Pvt. of Co. H all decided to risk the ultimate military penalty and fled their unit.

Fredericksburg just across the river from them was a quiet, small city of about 5,000 people. It also was strategically about half way in a direct line from Washington to Richmond. By late November, Burnside had demanded the civil authorities of Fredericksburg surrender the city, and Lee had told them he could not protect the city, and had recommended its evacuation. By the time of the battle it was all but deserted of civilians. This was the setting for this great battle about to commence. The valley at that location is not too wide, with sloping heights rising from both banks of the river. Those immediately behind Fredericksburg were called Marye's Heights. By December 10th they were studded with formidable defenses of rifle pits, stone walls and multiple artillery batteries, all well placed for effective defense. The Rebel artillery could not command the river itself, but south of the town was a gently sloping open field of about one half mile leading up to the heights, and clearly the artillery could command those approaches.

Finally, Burnside's plan was ready on December 10th, and orders went out that day for movement on the 11th. The plan called for three pontoon bridges to be thrown over the river nearly simultaneously on the early morning of the 11th. Franklin's Grand Division was to cross downstream, with the intent of skirting the heights, attack the enemy's right, disrupt it, and when that had occurred, for Sumner's Grand Division, including most of the Ninth Corps, having moved across the bridges into Fredericksburg proper, would attack the heights. Franklin's forces were the largest with about 36,000 men, Sumner's about 26,000. Backing both up was to be Hooker's Grand Division, to move wherever needed. The 89th was detailed in Sumner's forces, Ninth Corps with General Orlando B. Willcox in command, the Third Division under General George Getty, the First Brigade under the command of Col. Rush Hawkins, of the Ninth NYVI. There were five other regiments in the brigade, namely the 10th and 13th New Hampshire, the 25th New Jersey and the 9th and 103rd NY regiments.

Early the morning of the 11th of December with all in readiness, the pontoon trains arrived at their respective sites. The work was to be carried out by the engineer regiments with infantry units crouched on the north shore to protect and cover their work. The morning was cold and damp, cold enough to have thin ice on the river before them. In the course of the middle bridge deployment, sited near the railroad crossing, the 89th was selected to be the supporting infantry. The work commenced before dusk, and was proceeding well. The middle bridge was under construction by the 50th NY Engineers, but with light the sharpshooters and riflemen arrayed on the south bank, secreted in rifle pits, in homes near the shore, and in the basements of homes began to annoy the work progress. Before long, the work at first just dangerous became deadly. In spite of artillery fire directed at the homes suspected of housing the Rebel riflemen, and the musket fire of the 89th infantrymen, there was little pause in the fire of the rebels. The Union artillerists on the Stafford Heights reported difficulty directing fire accurately because of a fog that had formed in the valley that morning, combined with the smoke of burning buildings in the city. The unarmed engineers ceased there work, waited for volleys of supporting fire, and then would try again, but only to meet the same deadly Rebel fire. Finally in the afternoon, General Burnside ordered that Colonel Fairchild have 100 of his men, led by four officers, cross in boats to attack and dislodge the hidden sharpshooters. The officers were Captains Hazley, Judd, and Burt, and Lieutenant Lewis. Each officer had in his boat twenty-five men from the 89th, the boats being crewed by men of the 50th Engineers. These men in the pontoon boats faced murderous musket fire from the south shore, but managed to get across, leapt out of their boats, and led by the four officers, rapidly attacked and captured the hiding places of the sharpshooters. In this action, four officers and sixty men from the Rebel emplacements were captured, and the south shore was secured in this area. After the battle was over, there was talk in the camps that the men involved would be honored with medals. Even officers claimed that General Burnside made that promise. As history unfolded, there never were medals for these brave men, but the incident was a high, bright point in the annals of the 89th.

After the advance of the 89th had crossed and done their deeds, the remainder of the 89th crossed likewise in boats, while the middle bridge was being completed, then in relative safety. The 89th was ordered to move into the city and secure it, and was one of the first units to occupy Fredericksburg. During the afternoon and evening of the 11th, most of the rest of the Army crossed the bridges, and arrayed itself for the coming assaults. The 89th was on the left of the Union line by the 12th. During that day, the 12th of December, there was shameful looting and destruction of the homes and businesses of the people of the suffering City of Fredericksburg, largely uncontrolled by the officers of the Union army. There was little military action that day as Burnside went over more details of the planned assault, and as Lee further fortified his defenses, and shifted his personnel to meet his foe most efficiently.

Early on the morning of the 13th of December, Franklin's wing, the largest in this army, was to attack the right of the Confederate forces, where Jackson's Corps were waiting. This was a little southeast of town near Prospect Hill. The only unit however that got into action early was that division led by General Meade, and they succeeded in breaching the first line of defense in the woods, but having no real support, they were driven back by Rebel reserves. Burnside later testified that he repeatedly directed Franklin to get his entire command into action, but there was no haste in getting this enacted by General Franklin, and eventually the action on the Union left failed. This also meant that there was no disruption from the flank to the main body of the Rebel defenders on the heights south of the city. Sumner's wing now faced the enemy across open ground sloping upward towards the entrenched forces of General Longstreet, fully prepared to meet the attacks, and eager for the opportunity to defend their homeland.

Sumner had General Darius Couch's Corps with General French's Division commencing the attacks. This started about eleven AM, and was slow to pick up momentum, as the Union forces slowly drove Confederate pickets away. When the pickets retreated behind their works, the attacks began in earnest. Union artillery attempted to soften the works with barrage after barrage, but their firing did not have the desired effect. French's forces gallantly attacked and were repulsed, and these men were followed by the division led by General Winfield Hancock, who likewise failed to reach the Confederate positions. The next wave was led by General Oliver Howard with a similar fate.

The last charges of the day were those of General Orlando Willcox's divisions, but by the time this had all transpired through the deadly day of fighting, the brief December daylight was nearly gone. Willcox first had the division under General Sturgis attack, and like all before, that one failed, and the final assault of the 13th of December was made by General Getty's Division, including the 89th. They formed and moved south across the old canal bed, through a marshy area. Their target was the right of the heights (near the present day National Cemetery). Some elements of the Ninth Corps succeeded in getting to within about ten yards of the stone wall and held that position under exposed fire for up to seven futile minutes before being withdrawn by General Getty. While in that forward position, they were nearly surrounded by musket fire from their front, from the flanks, and even from their rear. By this time, the Confederate defenders in this vicinity of the battlefield included General Thomas Cobb's Brigade of Georgian Regiments (16th, 18th and 24th), a part of General LaFayette McLaw's Division; portions of General J.R.Cooke's Brigade of North Carolinian Regiments (apparently the 25th, the 24th having been withdrawn shortly before the final assault), a portion of Ransom's Division; and these had been joined by portions of General James Kemper's Brigade of Virginians (1st, 3rd, 7th, 11th, and 24th), loaned from Pickett's Division further to the right. All of these were under the immediate command of Brigadier General Robert Ransom, Jr. Meanwhile, straggler elements of the 83rd PA and 20th ME regiments had taken some shelter after their own attack failed, and were returning fire on the Confederates, but some of this fire was inadvertently aimed at their own comrades, the last assaulting units, who had gotten in between during their charge. The final attack failed, as had all the prior ones of the day.

And, with the last charge over, the fighting ceased with the darkness, and the 89th retreated to the town. On the 14th, Burnside contemplated another round of assaults, but these never materialized. During the 14th , the 89th held a position near Caroline Street. On the 15th, all of the forces were withdrawn back across the river to the north bank. The great battle was over.

The Confederate Army units actually engaged on the 13th of December on the heights south of Fredericksburg were only a small portion of General Longstreet's whole command. The number has been estimated at about 5,000. Many of the Rebel casualties were from Union artillery barrages. Total losses for the three days from the Confederate forces were reported by the Medical Director on January the 10th 1863 as having been 458 killed and 3,743 wounded men. The Confederate reports seldom detail missing or captured men, so this number is hard to ascertain. Of the total though, the best numbers for casualties on the heights, the focus of the repeated Union assaults, showed that there were 20 killed and 486 wounded. The Union losses were staggering in comparison. The Ninth Corps alone, which included the 89th , had 8 officers and 103 men killed, and 44 officers and 1,023 men wounded. In the right grand division of Sumner, there were 62 officers killed, 310 wounded and 1 missing, while there were 461 enlisted men killed, 3,971 wounded, and there were a total of 639 soldiers missing. The whole of the Army of the Potomac for the battle had 1,284 soldiers killed and 9,600 soldiers wounded. There were reports of 1,769 missing. Confederate reports indicated about 900 prisoners from the battle.

The 89th had losses of 4 killed (including Dean Van Buren, Wagoner of Co. C, who was killed on the 11th). Two of these four died later from wounds. Twenty five men were listed as wounded (including Pvts. Clinton Earnest of Co. G and probably David Johnson of Co. F, and poor Pvt. Willis Humfrey of Co. C, previously wounded at Antietam and then back in action with his unit) and 1 missing. General Burnside's only major battle as the Chief Union General was a disaster in the eyes of historians. While one more major assault was planned by General Burnside, weather, not enemy soldiers defeated that effort. The Mud March was Burnside's last attempt at crushing the Rebel forces, but the sticky red clay roads of the then wintery Virginia made the movement of an entire Army impossible. The Army of the Potomac could muster no further serious action that winter. Burnside was disgraced and replaced in January of 1863.

1863

In February of 1863, the 89th left northern Virginia and moved to the vicinity of Newport News, Virginia. They were out of tents again, this time in log barracks. Their status was rather comfortable, but short-lived. They were in this area until moved to Suffolk. They arrived in that region on March 14 as reinforcement for the men of the 7th Corps already there. Here they contructed and manned defensive positions.

The Siege of Suffolk
(for correlation, see the letters dated from March 15th to May, 1863)

Suffolk, Virginia, some 30 miles from Norfolk, had been held by Union forces as something of an advance position to protect Norfolk and to watch Rebel movements in the peninsula between the James and Albermarle waterways. Suffolk, at the head of the Nansemond River was a small city but important as the junction point of two Virginia railways, the Petersburg and Norfolk, and the Seaboard and Roanoke. Suffolk was also flanked on its east by the great Dismal Swamp, which afforded a formidable natural barrier to movement. That spring the Union forces were under the command of Major General John J. Peck. There were rumors and some intelligence indicating that Lieutenant General Longstreet was planning an attack on Suffolk, with the ultimate goal of liberating Norfolk. This would have permited the Confederate ironclads to work against the Union blockade and open the James waterway back up to the relief of the interior of Virginia.

On April 11th of 1863 a large force of Confederates arrived and promptly overran advanced posts of the Union defenders. The forces of the Confederate Army here, under the command of the veteran Gen. Longstreet was in the neighborhood of 30,000 men. Later with the consolidation of his forces and the arrival of troops from North Carolina, the number may have been 38,000 men. The Union defense had considerably fewer men. Early in March the number was probably about 9,000 in the area, but by late March it was more on the order of 15,000. By the end of the Siege, the defense had been reinforced to about 29,000 Union soldiers. These were spread over a defense radius of works amounting to almost 15 miles.

A significant assault on April 11th followed the capture of the outposts, but an alarm had been effectively given, and the Northern forces repulsed the attacks that day. Over the next several days, probing attacks on the flanks of the defenses failed to find fundamental weaknesses, and before long the larger army of the Southerners laid siege on the defenses of Suffolk. Officially, the Siege of Suffolk took place April 11 through May 4, 1863, and the 89th was involved in two important aspects of this action. They were posted in one of the concentrated defensive areas, locally called forts, and theirs was a secondary line of defense. They were part of the division of Gen. Getty which held a difficult and nearly eight mile section of the defense. He reported that his men created nearly 8,000 yards of rifle pits and nearly 2,000 feet of parapets seven feet high, cut 10 miles of new road and created several bridges for passage over small creeks and swamp areas.

But, on April 19th a detachment of the 89th was instrumental in the spectacular capture of a Confederate position. Rebel artillery commanders posted batteries, after the April 11th sweeping of Union positions away from the west bank of the Nansemond, at various locations in order to counter Union gunboat effectiveness and hopefully command the river. They also regularly shelled Union defenses on the opposite banks. On April 14th one of the gunboats, the Mount Washington, was severely damaged in its movements on the river, and the other gunboats were withdrawn to safer locations. This left the eastern bank of the Nansemond at higher risk of a successful Rebel crossing and assault. General Getty and Lieutenant Lamson of the Navy concocted a plan to capture the battery on Hill's Point. This battery was behind earthen works and was staffed by men of the Fauquier Artillery under the command of Captain Robert Stribling. There were two companies of infantry attached to and protecting the battery, with plans for rapid aide from other nearby infantry in the event of attack by Yankee soldiers. The men at the battery were from Companies A and B of the 44th Alabama Infantry. There were three 12 lb. cannons and two 20 lb. cannons in this battery, which were arrayed towards the river. On the evening of April 19th six companies of the 8th Conn Regiment, 130 men in all, together with about 150 men of the 89th, under the command of Lt. Col. England, embarked on the gunboat Stepping Stones. Lieut. Lamson accompanied with four small boat howitzers. The gunboat landed about 300 yards from the battery, the men scrambled ashore through the mud and attacked the battery from behind. In very short order the 5 cannon were captured along with officers and men of the artillery including Captain Stribling totalling 59, and at least 71 infantrymen including 5 officers. The Union advance was quickly reinforced and converted to a defensive position for an expected Rebel counterattack. This counterattack did not occur that night or even the next day, but the Union forces were withdrawn on the night of the 20th with the Confederates never really menacing. The action freed the gunboats for return activity on that portion of the Nansemond, and effectively on others too, as two other river batteries were withdrawn by the Confederates to prevent similar surprise capture. The capture of this battery was a disappointment and embarrassment to the Southerners and a great deal of finger-pointing as to responsibility and blame ensued after the event.

The Union loss in this highly successful assault was 4 dead and 10 wounded. Of this number, two of the dead (Jehial Smith, Pvt. of Co. F and Lt. Marvin Watrous of Co. B) and six of the wounded (including Pvt. Charles Fiske, Co. F who died three days later and possibly William Utter, Pvt. of Co. F) were from the 89th detachment. During the next several days the 89th remaineded in its positions, the men mainly in rifle pits, but in good spirits.

On May third, General Getty ordered a reconnaisance of the region along the Providence Church Road. The 89th and 103rd NY regiments led the movement. As they advanced, they overran a number of positions. There were no causalties in the 89th that day according to official reports, yet we know from other records that there were three wounded men of Co. I, namely Pvt. John Davidson, who made a miraculous recovery only to die convalescing at home in Delaware Co.; Pvt. John Thompson, and Lt. Henry Epps; and also Pvt. Whitney Moore of Co. G who was discharged for his disability some six months later. On the night of May third, the Confederates abandoned all of their siege positions and withdrew back towards the Blackwater River. The Siege of Suffolk was over. Norfolk was safe for the time. In the siege, the 89th had a total of 3 killed (the other not named above may have been Pvt. John Clemens of Co. D) and 10 wounded.

In late May, the troops were on the move again, this time to a camp nearer Norfolk, Virginia. From here, they were part of the 1863 peninsular movements, mindful of the defeats in the same regions the year before. By late July there was talk of the drafted men coming to fill the depleted ranks, and camp life was again routine, then suddenly on July 31st, they found themselves on board ship again, this time aboard the Adalaide, and ended in the Charleston Harbor region.

From their base on Folly Island, the unit was involved in the support of the various actions against the installations in Charleston Harbor, including Battery Wagner and the siege of Fort Sumpter. During their time in South Carolina, the 89th was transferred from the old Ninth Corps to the Tenth Corps. While in this theater they were not involved in combat. There were a number of deaths from disease however. The water quality and sanitation on the island were at times very poor, and diarrheal illnesses were common. Some of the men who died on Folly Island were: Pvts. Harvey Davis of Co. E, George Durfee of Co. H, and Ransom Frost of Co. G; Sgt. Ira Jacobs of Co. I; Pvts. Delos Letts and Isaac Swallow of Co. A, John Sweet of Co. B, James Watrous of Co. G; and Monroe Williams of Co. K.

They were in the region until later April of 1864 when they were moved back to Virginia. Sometime in the spring of 1864, the new recruits were arriving to fill the companies, some badly depleted by the ravages of war and disease. It is unlikely that there was much drill time for these men who were about to experience the life of the infantryman in earnest.

1864

Richmond Campaign
(for correlation, see letters 5/8/64, 5/18/64, 5/21/64 and 5/28/64)

In April, the 89th left South Carolina and joined the massing troops on the southeastern part of Virginia. Early in May they were part of the grand design of General Benjamin Butler's campaign to attack Richmond from behind Lee's Army, then facing the forces of Grant and Meade further to the north. Butler, with nearly 30,000 men was to move up the south side of the James River, and invest Richmond from the south. The Confederate forces there were under the command of General G. T. Beauregard, who happened still to be in North Carolina with most of his troops, and the total number of defenders for the South early in May was just some 3000 men (including War Department clerks), with another 2000 defending Petersburg. As history has shown however, Butler barely moved, and missed any opportunity to meet his major objective. A secondary objective was the destruction of the railroad between Richmond and Petersburg to its south. This was only partly accomplished and never to a damaging point. Instead, the expedition holed up defensively, rather than pursuing the offensive, in a position only a few miles east of the Richmond to Petersburg turnpike and railroad, and only fifteen miles from Richmond. General Beauregard used the Union ineptitude to bring up men totalling close to 20,000, and himself went on the offensive against Butler's forces. Although the Union lines were secured, it then was easy for Beauregard to envelope and contain the Union 'invaders', who moved back to near Bermuda Hundred. General Beauregard was even able to send badly needed men to Lee.

The 89th was in the second division under General John Turner, of the Tenth Army Corps commanded by General Quincy Gillmore. They were involved in several of the skirmishes of this campaign, but the only official casualties occurred at the one called Proctor's Creek on May 12th. Here 5 enlisted men were wounded, and one was killed. The wounded included Pvt. James Little and Cpl. Thomas Thompson of Co. I.

Cold Harbor
(see the letters of June 9 and 11, 1864)

On May 30th, the 89th was among units transferred from the 10th to the 18th Corps. Now, in the second division under General John Martindale, they were assigned to the first brigade under General George Stannard. They were transferred to the Army of the Potomac and moved towards Cold Harbor, Virginia. Grant and Lee had been shifting and moving from the Wilderness, through Spotsylvania and Totopotomoy, and on June 1st ended up near Cold Harbor.

There on June 3, another great disaster for the Union forces ensued when forces, principally those of General Hancock, assaulted the well constructed works of the rebels, and met disasterous fire. For a week or so after, trench warfare with artillery and sniper fire abounding was the order of the action. Fortunately, the 89th was not among the units decimated in the attacks of June third, but did suffer some casualties in the days following, while in the works. Some of the works for the Union were as close as forty yards from those of the Confederates. Anyone exposing himself or even his head in those forward positions was literally risking his life during the long June daylight hours. During those twelve days in June, three enlisted men were killed outright (including Lawrence Kain, Cpl. of Co. H) and two more died of wounds. Among those dead from fighting at Cold Harbor were Winfield Carrier, Pvt. of Co. H, who had enlisted less than four and a half months earlier; Clinton Hart, Pvt. of Co.E; and Sgt. Thomas Hepesaul of Co. G. Thirteen others were wounded but recovered. These latter included Pvt. Jackson Dyer of Co. F; Cpl. Jacob King of Co. F; and Sgt. James Mahew of Co. H. Two men were reported as missing and these probably were Wilson Dean, a Pvt. of Co. A and William Law, a Pvt. of Co. I.

Petersburgh
(for correlation, see letters dated 6/25/64 through 8/18/64)

When it was clear to Grant that frontal assaults on a well entrenched enemy was not an answer to the destruction of Lee's army, he decided to withdraw. On the 12th of June, 1864 the largest part of the army left the rifle pits and the artillery positions at Cold Harbor. The army was going to attempt a rapid movement, to come from the south of Richmond before Lee could ascertain and adapt to the new position. This next major battle was another of the stunning failures to execute what seemed to be sound military strategy, and again the 89th was along for the ride.

The plan looked in mid June as if it might be a success, as by June 15th Grant's army was south of the James, with Lee's still north of the James, and just then learning where the Federal army had moved to. Back at Petersburg, then a great rail hub, the Confederates numbered only about 2000 men, with 7000 more still down near Bermuda Hundred keeping Butler's men in check (see above under the Richmond campaign). General Smith, with the 89th being a part, was in the lead, and as the outmanned General Beauregard, still the commander of the Confederates of the region, testified after the war, Petersburg was all but captured at that time, only the Union generals failed again to capitalize on their strength. Smith's attacks on the 15th actually broke the defenses, but there was no further movement, in fact, the orders from General Smith to his troops were to build defensive positions again. On the 16th of June, there were nearly 50,000 Union soldiers in the immediate vicinity, and now there were about 9,000 Rebel defenders, but incredibly, the attacks did not come until evening, and were barely repulsed. The effects of the delays were the obvious though, that is that Lee had time to get his army south just in time.

On the 17th, the attacks were enough to break the defensive lines, but General Beauregard skillfully pulled his men back to and held a secondary defensive line closer towards the city. On the 18th, the attacks again were miserably coordinated, and in fact did not occur in many areas along the line until just after Lee's army poured into the poorly defended, and in some spots undefended works. In general, the attacks of the 18th of June were failures. By that night, the city of Petersburg was behind strong Confederate defenses, and the two armies once again faced each other across no-man's land from the partial safety of rifle pits and supporting trenches.

The 89th was initially a part of the first brigade, under General George Stannard, then the third brigade under General Adelbert Ames, but each time in the Second Division, commanded by General John Martindale, of the 18th Army Corps. This was the Corps under General Smith, which had made up the lead elements of the assaults on the first day's attacks near Petersburg. On the 15th for instance, the brigade led by General Stannard was the lead element of the attack in one area, and captured works near the Appomatox River. The detailed record for the 15th through the 18th of June is very sketchy in regards to the second division, so we are not aware of the actions of the 89th during those early days of the Petersburg campaign. Clapper Eldridge (one of the new recruits) and James Groves, Pvts. of Co. H; Albert Lybolt, Pvt. Co. A; Benjamin Rosselle and William Snow, Pvts. in Co. H; and Eliphalet Weed, Jr., a Pvt of Co A all were killed in the first three days' actions. Also on June 16th, supposedly just after an assault, Lt. Col. Theophilus England was killed, shot through the head. Reportedly, he was ministering to a wounded Rebel soldier when shot, and he died instantly. Some of the wounded in this phase from the 89th included Seymour Judd, Capt. of Co. G wounded on the 16th, but who died a little over two months later; Silas Manning, Pvt. of Co. A; Delos Payne, Pvt. of Co.F (and another new recruit) who died of his wounds just under two months later; Charles Peck, Pvt. of Co. C; George Pittsley, a Pvt. of Co. F who died on June 18th; and Pliney Russell, Cpl. of Co. G.

By the 18th of June, the 18th Corps was relieved of their forward positions. Later in the month, portions were sent back to Gen. Butler's lines temporarily. During the month of July, the 89th was assigned to the rifle pits, two days in and two days on reserve away from the front. Then, on July 29, they received orders to move to be in support of a planned major assault, to be carried out by Gen. Burnside's Ninth Corps.

This, another in a whole series of Union miscues, mistakes or lost opportunities, fortunately did not affect the 89th much that day. On July 31st a large explosion set off in a mine dug beneath a series of Confederate works was to be the focal point for a assault onto and then over the Rebel defenses of Petersburg. The assault began well, but hesitated, then sputtered to a stop, and ended with southern fire into the massed northern men in the crater, like shooting fish in a barrel. The 89th witnessed the explosion, but were not called on to move forward.

The failure of the Crater, as it has been called, left the two sides in the siege warfare again. More men of the 89th lost their lives in these later activities, including Elijah Atwater and Samuel Fitch, Pvts. of Co. K; Hiram Foster, Pvt of Co. H; Albert Jones, Pvt. of Co. I; Mason Smith, Pvt. of Co. G; and Lucius Traver, a Pvt. of Co. C. Wounded men in this trench warfare included James Mallan, a Pvt. of Co. B, and Abisha Stephens, a Pvt. of Co. G.

The stunning successes of the Southern army in the spring to summer campaign in Virginia were enormous, but came at a different kind of price. The move to protect Petersburg that followed Grant's move south also kept Lee's army bottled up in close contact with Grant's army for the rest of the war. Their inability to get out and manuever also meant that they never again could threaten outside their Capitol region. General Lee's hopes had to be distant ones, relying on General Hood in the Georgia and Tennessee regions to try to defeat Generals Sherman and Thomas, and on General Early in the Shenandoah Valley fighting General Sheridan to keep that line of supply and support open. If there had been major victory by the Southerners in either realm, then the pressure might come off Lee. In the end, of course, each of these failed, and the hopes for a Confederate victory of one army against another with it. Even so, and unfortunately for the Union forces around Petersburg and Richmond, there was still war to fight where they were, and the 89th faced severe trials yet.

By August of 1864 many of the men of the 89th could do little else but dream of the end of their three-year terms, just weeks away. Some few men had re-enlisted, enticed by the huge bounties offered by the governments to do so, and the recruits were settling into the company they were assigned to, but the character of the regiment was much changed. After nearly three years of battle and disease, relatively few of the original men were left. Many probably hoped to coast out their last few weeks in some reserve capacity, but the war would not let them be.

Chaffin's Farm/Fort Harrison/Fort Gilmer

Late in September of 1864, north of the James, the Union army added another of the series of movements against the Confederate positions. On the 28th, the Eighteenth Army Corps, General Edward Ord commanding, crossed the river James at night with portions of the Tenth Army Corps, to prepare assaults against Rebel positions. General Charles Heckman commanded the second division, in which the 89th NYVI was a part of the third brigade, which was led by Col. Fairchild at this juncture. The second division was to skirt easterly through the edge of woods to come at Fort Harrison from the east, just after the first division was to have taken the fort across the open approach. The first division accomplished their goal of storming and capturing the fort. The second division however got broken in the woods, the brigades separated, and were delayed in getting into action. This, as is often the case, let the defending Confederates be better prepared, and the attack on the neighboring Fort Gilmer was repulsed.

In this action, the 89th had 3 men killed (including John Poole, Pvt. of Co. E, and Joseph White, Pvt. of Co. G); 1 officer and 15 men wounded (including Willard Blinebry, Cpl. Co. I, who was captured and paroled, but who died three weeks later of his wound; Sgt. Harvey How of Co. F, who died the same day; John Mallon, Pvt. of Co. B; and possibly Stephen Lawrence, Pvt. of Co. A), and had 3 officers (Lt. Henry Epps of Co. I; Lt. Thomas Groody of Co. B; and Capt. Henry Roome of Co. E); and 17 men (including Hiram Brown, Pvt. Co. I; George Folmsbee, Pvt. of Co. A; Henry Foote, Pvt. of Co. K; Cpl. Daniel Mains of Co. I; and John Reed, Pvt. of Co. E) missing. The Eighteenth Corps had a total of 2,328 casualties, which included the death of Gen. Hiram Burnham leading his brigade of the first division, and the wounding of the Corps commander, General Ord. It was a difficult day for the men of the 89th, many with only one month to go in their terms.

The Confederate troops that the 89th faced on the September 29th were probably of General Charles W. Field's division of Longstreet's Corps, and the indications of later reports are that they faced principally General Maxcy Gregg's brigade, composed of the Third Arkansas, as well as the 1st, 4th and 5th Texas Regiments. The Rebel entrenchments may also have been manned by General John Bratton's brigade of South Carolina men from the 1st, 2nd, 5th, 6th Regiments, and the Palmetto Sharpshooters. Later in the day reinforcements included units of Pickett's Corps and R.H. Anderson's Division of Longstreet's First Army Corp. Casualty reports are not available for these units. On the following day, Confederate troops massed for and made an assault on Fort Harrison to try to retake it, but this attack failed. After this battle, the Eighteenth Corps took positions in the trenches to the side of Fort Harrison, which they occupied most of the month of October.

The Battle of Fair Oaks

On October 26th, just days after the completion of the mustering-out of the three years men of the 89th, the Eighteenth Corps, now under the command of General Godfrey Weitzel, left their positions in the works near Fort Harrison, (renamed Fort Burnham in honor of the fallen General in charge of its capture the month before). Many of the regiment had been mustered into the service the same month, and had very little, if any, drilling or battlefield experience. These men would have had to rely on the hardy veteran troops in their midst. They marched with three days rations towards Seven Pines, crossing at the head of White Oak Swamp. They met Rebel forces strongly posted behind their fortifications near Fair Oaks, where a battle ensued. This was very near the ground of the Battle of Fair Oak previously. About two in the afternoon, battle lines were formed, and the third brigade, commanded by Col. Fairchild, of the second division, now led by General Charles A. Heckman, was designated the charging party along with Col. Cullen's brigade of the first division. This battle, for the 89th, was to be one of the saddest in their military history.

About 4 PM, the third brigade, composed of the 19th Wisconsin and 89th and 148th NY regiments valiantly charged the works, across about 800 yards of open ground, but found them much too strong to take by storm. Those in the front managed to reach about 150 yards from the entenchments, facing withering fire, but got no further. The men did not flee, but took slight shelter in something of a gully, and remained until there was an order to retreat. Then the shattered remnants of the brigade formed a new line with Col. Fairchild, and collected as many of the wounded men as they could. Sometime about five in the late afternoon, the Confederates sallied forth from their fortifications and captured large numbers of the Union forces of the two advance brigades along with six regimental colors. To the credit of the color sergeant Smith of the 89th, the regimental flag was restored to the regiment.

By then, darkness was coming on, and to add to the misery of the day, it rained as well. The 18th Corps retired that night, and wearily marched back to the same works they had occupied a couple of days before, the last unit arriving at 4 PM on the 28th of October.

In the action of the 27th, the second division losses were three officers and nine enlisted men killed, seven officers and ninety one men wounded, and six officers and three hundred and eighty men missing. Of this total, the casualties to the 89th were as follows: 2 officers (these were Lt. Col. Wellington Lewis, who died in May of 1865 materially from that wound and 1st Lt. Albert Burt of Co. K) and 3 enlisted men killed, and four other enlisted men who were wounded later died of their wounds; 1 officer (Lt. George Hughes of Co. K) and 32 enlisted men were wounded (including Pvts. John Mann and Charles Scott of Co. C, and Pvt. Charles Loomis of Co. A), but recovered. Ninety eight men were missing in this battle, leading to an aggregate loss to the regiment of 139. The men known to have been captured are listed in Table form.

Table: Captured at Fair Oaks

Soldier	Company	Veteran	Rank	Release
Baker, Adolf	A	N	Pvt.	Paroled
Barrick, James	F	N	Pvt.	May 1865
Brown, Edward	K	N	Pvt.	Paroled
Brown, Edward M.	K	N	Pvt.	Paroled
Burns, Edward	K	N	Pvt.	Paroled
Carmichael, Tho.	K	N	Pvt.	Paroled
Collins, James	F	N	Pvt.	Paroled
Corbett, Timothy	K	N	Pvt.	Paroled
Covert, Abram	K	Y	Pvt.	Paroled
Daly, Frances	D	N	Pvt.	Unknown
Debau, William	K	N	Pvt.	Paroled
Deery, Edward	F	N	Pvt.	Paroled
Douglass, Charles	K	N	Pvt.	Paroled
Dumas, David	A	N	Pvt.	Paroled
Essler, John	D	N	Pvt.	2/28/65
Florence, James	K	N	Pvt.	Paroled
Frost, John	K	N	Pvt.	Paroled
Harmin, Frank	K	N	Pvt.	Paroled
Harrin, Albert	K	N	Pvt.	Paroled
Harrington, Wm.	F	N	Pvt.	2/6/65

Harris, Henry	K	N	Pvt.	died 1/65
Held, George	K	N	Pvt.	Paroled
Hickey, John	K	N	Pvt.	Paroled
Hinch, John	K	N	Pvt.	Paroled
Hoffman, George	K	N	Pvt.	Paroled
Kavannagh, Sylvester	K	N	Pvt.	Paroled
Kity, William	K	N	Pvt.	Paroled
Knapp, George	A	N	Pvt.	Paroled
Lamb, Rodman	F	N	Pvt.	Paroled
Latourno, Joseph	A	N	Pvt.	Unknown
Lawrence, Charles	K	N	Pvt.	Paroled
Martin, John	A	N	Pvt.	Unknown
McGinness, Arthur	F	N	Pvt.	Paroled
McKee, John	K	N	Pvt.	Paroled
Moore, Samuel	K	N	Pvt.	Paroled
Myers, Henry	D	N	Pvt.	Unknown
Myre, John	A	N	Pvt.	Unknown
Nelson, H. S.	K	N	Pvt.	Paroled
Newton, George	H	N	Pvt.	5/1/65
Patterson, George	K	N	Pvt.	Paroled
Patzack, Charles	A	N	Pvt.	Unknown
Pixley, Lorenzo	F	N	Pvt.	Unknown
Purnell, George	K	N	Pvt.	Paroled
Reilly, Michael	D	N	Pvt.	Paroled
Rossiter, Edward	A	N	Pvt.	Unknown
Ryan, Patrick	D	N	Pvt.	Unknown
Sharp, William	K	N	Pvt.	Paroled
Smith, John	F	N	Pvt.	Paroled
Solomon, Solomon	A	N	Pvt.	Paroled
Specht, Joseph	A	N	Pvt.	Paroled
Stewart, William	K	N	Pvt.	Paroled
Stone, Peter	A	N	Pvt.	Unknown
Strain, William	K	N	Pvt.	Paroled
Stringham, George	B	Y	Pvt.	Paroled
Thomas, David	I	Y	Pvt.	Unknown
Wagner, George	D	N	Pvt.	Unknown
Zends, Erhardt	K	N	Pvt.	Paroled

Of the men captured at the second battle near Fair Oaks in the 89th, only three were veterans and moreover forty five of the men listed in the table above were mustered into the service of the Union army less than four weeks before this battle. Clearly, this was not a charge made by battle-experienced soldiers. Patrick Ryan, as an example, was mustered into Company D's service on October 13th, exactly two weeks prior to the ill-fated charge. It is thought that several of the men captured were also wounded, but the records are not clear on this point. In his report dated October 31st about the operation of October 27th, Brevet Major General Godfrey Weitzel, the commander of the Eighteenth Army Corps at the time took blame for the failure. He stated that he had personally reviewed the enemy works and felt they were defended only by three pieces of artillery and a relatively small number of men, actually dismounted cavalry. He also felt that the delay between his order to attack and the actual attack time left the Confederated forces too long to reinforce, and prepare for the attack.

In fact, the rebel forces were prepared for the attack. General Longstreet had ordered the divisions under Generals Field and Robert Hoke to move into defensive positions anticipating the area of attack. The area along the Williamsburg Road that Colonel Fairchild's Third Brigade attacked was defended by the division under General Field. Casualty reports for Field's division for the 27th have a total of 64, of which total only 9 were reported killed. General Longstreet reported nearly 600 Federal soldiers captured. Eleven stands of Union colors were captured, and many of these were taken by the 5th South Carolina regiment. The 5th South Carolina was a part of Bratton's Brigade of Field's division, although General Bratton was not in command at the time of this battle. His brigade was led that day by Col. Joseph Walker, of the Palmetto Sharpshooters.

1865

During the later fall of 1864 and early winter of 1865, the activity of the 89th while remaining in the Petersburg and Richmond vicinity, did not involve much combat. The Union forces were able to vote in the 1864 Presidential election which brought Old Abe back for another term. Both armies in the area waited for news of fighting particularly in Tennessee and Georgia, and the 89th, transferred to the new Twenty Fourth Corps in December, probably celebrated the news of the capture of Savannah at Christmas time with the rest of the Northern citizens, and the fall of Charleston in February. And, when General Sherman's forces began their long move north to join with General Grant, and when General Johnston determined that he could do no more than annoy General Sherman, the Union forces knew they were moving towards the final push. The stage was set for the last major fighting of the long and bloody Civil War, which had already taken the lives of more than 600,000 Americans.

Appomattox Campaign

Some overtures for peace were cast in that late winter of 1865, and President Lincoln hoped for an end with no further bloodbaths, but General Grant believed that one more major conflict was in the offing. The Confederates held on to slim hopes, although morale was very poor, desertions were very high, and new recruitment was almost non-existent. Still, as long as there were supply routes open, the Rebels were entrenched behind formidable defensive works. Late in March, the Union forces prepared for a spring assault on Petersburg. In the meantime, Lee assigned General John Gordon to try to punch through Grant's defenses at Fort Stedman. The Federals rallied after being taken by surprise, and crushed the attack. This then was the last offensive move that Lee's army made.

The first division of the 24th Army crossed the James River from the north bank and then crossed the Appomatax River, and on the 29th of March of 1865, arrived near Hatcher's Run. On the 30th and 31st this division drove the confederates back from advanced lines to their main lines, moving ever closer to the last defense of Petersburg. General Grant called for a general assault against Petersburg on April second. The 24th Army Corps under General John Gibbon had the assignment of assaulting some works in the protection of Petersburg, and as it turned out their assignment was one of the toughest ones of the day. The 89th was a part of the fourth brigade of the first division under General Robert Foster and the brigade commander was Col. Harrison Fairchild. The fourth brigade was composed of the 8th Maine, the 89th, 148th, and 158th New York, and the 55th Pennsylvania Regiments.

Fort Gregg was a palisaded earth and log structure with loopholes for muskets, and fronted by a kind of moat. There was artillery support for the defenders, and inside were stubborn and grim men. At about one in the afternoon the attack commenced, and gallantly the men charged into a hail of lead. As they struggled across the moat, and helped one another up the steep parapet, there was twenty minutes or so of hand to hand combat before the garrison of the fort was overwhelmed. As soon as Fort Gregg fell, the neighboring Fort Baldwin was evacuated and occupied by other troops. Many Union regiments claimed to be the first in the fort, but General Foster reported that he could not decide who should have been afforded the honor, as they happened almost simultaneously. The 89th made one of the claims of first colors in the captured fort. Once in the fort, there were 57 bodies of defenders counted.

In this action Major Frank Tremain, leading the 89th, was killed at the fort. Also killed were three enlisted men, which included George Vermilyea, a Pvt. of Co. H. Wounded men, numbering 10, included William Atwater, Pvt. of Co. F, who died a little over three weeks later, Pvt. John Conway of Co. K, Sgt. George Englis of Co. K, Pvt. Charles Mack of Co. H, and Pvt. William Schism of Co. F, who died on April 15th of his wounds.

On April third, Petersburg was found abandoned, and the first division was on the march in pursuit of the fleeing Army of Northern Virginia. They were on the march towards Lynchburg, and overtook the enemy near Rice's Station on the 6th of April. On that day, overrunning the positions of the enemy cost the 89th one man killed (Pvt. Elwood Gates of Co. H) and 11 wounded (including David Ramsey, a Pvt of Co. D).

On the 8th, they resumed the march, reaching Appomattox Station, and on the 9th were about four miles from Appomattox Courthouse. Here skirmishing ensued with the 89th in a lead position preparing for assault when the word came that hostilities had ceased. Lee had surrendered to Grant, and for the men of the Eighty Ninth New York Volunteer Infantry, the war was finally over. The unit stayed at Appomattox Courthouse until April 17th, and then over the next few days, the Twenty Fourth marched slowly back towards Richmond. They reached the city on April 25th, 1865, and encamped on the north side.

Over the next few months, the 89th had various duties including Provost assignments. The unit was officially mustered out of service at Richmond, Virginia on August 3, 1865, bringing to an end almost four years of toil and death for these New Yorkers in the defense of their country. Theirs was a small part in the whole of the war, but for these participants of the Eighty Ninth New York Volunteer Infantry this part represented some of the most profound experiences of their lives.

In the aggregate, the unit losses were as follows:
Killed in action: 4 officers and 49 enlisted men.
Died from wounds: 2 officers and 52 enlisted men.
Died of disease and accident: 1 officer and 158 enlisted men.
Of those who died, 13 were in the hands of the enemy at the time of death.

Colonel Fairchild

At the organization of the Regiment and indeed throughout its career of service in the Union Army, Harrison S. Fairchild was the Colonel of the 89th NYVI. This was a somewhat unusual occurence for a New York regiment with a story of nearly four years of military activity. At times he was a Brigade Commander, as for instance he was at South Mountain, part of the Siege of Suffolk, and the Appomattox Campaign. He led his men in several battles. On March 13, 1865, he was promoted to Brigadier General by Brevet for gallant and meritorious services during the war. He was mustered out of the service with the Regiment on August 3, 1865 in Richmond, Virginia.

Prior to the Civil War he worked in banking, first as a clerk, then as a teller and bookkeeper. Later, he was a private banker, and in 1854 he was the president of the New Rochester Bank. About the same time he built a home in Rochester. In 1856 he was an Alderman for the city from the twelfth ward.

Harrison Fairchild was a Captain of the Rochester Light Guard and for nearly ten years before the Civil War was the Colonel of the 54th New York Militia. He also held the posts of Secretary and Treasurer of the New York State Military Association.

Harrison Stiles Fairchild was born in Cazenovia, New York, the first son of Philo and his wife Nancy (Stiles) Fairchild. His father was a well to do farmer in Madison County. In 1838, shortly after his father died, Harrison moved to Rochester, New York. He married Electa Jane Williams, a daughter of Harry B. Williams, on March 14, 1844. Harrison and Electa eventually had three children.

After the Civil War, he worked even until his hospitalization as a stocks and bonds broker, a real estate agent, and a United States Pension Claims Agent. He may have assisted men formerly under his command in this latter position. He was respected by his men during war time and recalled fondly by men after the war. In 1894 he attended a general reunion of the Regiment held in Norwich, New York, where he was warmly applauded.

Harrison Stiles Fairchild died in a Rochester hospital on January 25th, 1901. An obituary appeared in the Rochester Democrat and Chronicle on the following day, naming him as the ranking general officer of the city at the time of his death. He is buried in the Mount Hope Cemetery in Rochester.

Appendix A

Men of Company I

This appendix, drawn on the NYS Adjutant General's Report, Phisterer's New York in the War of the Rebellion, an Assistant Surgeon's Reports, Civil War Discharges recorded at the Delaware County Clerk's Office, and supplemented by the time period writings of some soldiers and later personal communications, will attempt to detail what is known of the men of Company I of the 89th NYVI. When there is reference made to a soldier in the letters, that date is listed here as well.

Andrews, William - Age, 19 years. Enlisted, September 16, 1861 at Delhi to serve three years; mustered in as private October 21, 1861; re-enlisted as a veteran, January 14, 1864; mustered out with Company, August 3, 1865, at Richmond, VA.

Baxter, Lebbeus - Age, 18 years. Enlisted, September 16, 1861 at Delhi, to serve three years; mustered in as private, November 15, 1861. Discharged November 18, 1864.

Becker, William - Age, 21 years. Enlisted, September 16, 1861 at Delhi, to serve three years; mustered in as private, October 21, 1861; promoted corporal, no date; discharged October 21, 1864; also borne as Beker. Letter 11/25/61.

Blanchard, Charles - Age, 40 years. Enlisted, September 16, 1861 at Delhi, to serve three years; mustered in as sergeant, October 21, 1861; returned to ranks, no date; discharged for disability, October 26, 1863. Born in Delaware County, NY.

Blinebry, Willard - Age, 24 years. Enlisted, November 12, 1861 at Delhi, to serve three years; mustered in as private November 25, 1861; promoted corporal, no date; re-enlisted as veteran, January 4, 1864; died, October 17, 1864 at Annapolis, MD; also borne as William and Blimby. According to surgeon report, was wounded by a shell fragment on September 29, 1864 at Chaffin's Farm, Va., and says was taken prisoner and paroled. Letter 1/10/64.

Block, Leon - Age, 23 years. Enlisted, September 16, 1861 at Delhi, to serve three years; mustered in as private October 21, 1861;

discharged October 21, 1864; also borne as Black.

Bowne, Robert E. - Age, 18 years. Enlisted, September 16, 1861 at Delhi, to serve three years; mustered in as private, October 21, 1861; discharged, October 21, 1864.

Boyd, Orsamus - Age, 18 years. Enlisted, September 16, 1861 at Delhi, to serve three years; mustered in as corporal, October 21, 1861; discharged October 2, 1862, by reason of promotion to second lieutenant in the 144th NYVI.

Bronson, Andrew Burr - Age, 22 years. Enlisted, September 16, 1861 at Delhi, to serve three years; mustered in as private October 21, 1861; died March 10, 1862 at Roanoke Is., NC., of Typhoid Fever. Letter 3/13/62

Bronson, Horatio - Age, 26 years. Enlisted, September 16, 1861 at Delhi, to serve three years; mustered in as private October 21, 1861; discharged October 21, 1864.

Brown, Hiram - Age, 24 years. Enlisted, September 16, 1861 at Delhi, to serve three years; mustered in as private October 21, 1861; re-enlisted as veteran, January 5, 1864; captured, September 29, 1864 at Chaffin's Farm, VA; released North East Bridge, NC March 4, 1865; discharged June 21, 1865, at Annapolis, MD; also borne as Hiram O. Letters 1/19/63 and 1/10/64.

Butts, Edward - Age, 24 years. Enlisted, September 16, 1861 at Delhi, to serve three years; mustered in as privated October 21, 1861; discharged for disability February 25, 1863.

Butts, Solomon - Age, 18 years. Enlisted, September 16, 1861 at Delhi, to serve three years; mustered in as private, October 21, 1861; re-enlisted as veteran, January 4, 1864; mustered out with company, August 3, 1865 at Richmond, VA. Letters 1/19/63, 1/10/64 and 2/15/65.

Case, David E. - Age, 40 years. Enlisted, September 16, 1861 at Delhi, to serve three years; mustered in as privated, October 21, 1861; discharged for disability, December 3, 1862; also borne as Cass. Letters 5/18/62, 6/24/62 and 10/25/62.

Coon, Edward I. - Age, 18 years. Enlisted, September 16, 1861 at Delhi, to serve three years; mustered in as private October 21, 1861; discharged October 24, 1864. Born in Delhi, NY.

Cormack, Robert P. - Age 32 years. Enrolled, September 16, 1861, at Delhi, to serve three years; mustered in as first lieutenant of Co. A, October 31, 1861; transferred to Co. I, December 4, 1861; mustered in as captain, Co. A, December 2, 1864; also borne as Carmack. Commissioned captain, February 2, 1863, with rank from December 27, 1862, vice H. Pratt resigned. Letters 11/28/61, 3/15/62, 3/31/62, 4/8/62, 4/21/62, 5/9/62, 4/27/63, and 7/16/64.

Daugharty, James - Age 18 years. Enlisted at Preston, January 4, 1864, to serve three years; mustered in as private, January 13, 1864; mustered out with company, August 3, 1865, at Richmond, Va.; also borne as Daugherty

Davidson, John - Age, 24 years. Enlisted, September 16, 1861 at Delhi, to serve three years; mustered in as private October 21, 1861; discharged for disability, August 27, 1863. Born Delhi, NY. He was severely wounded in the abdomen at Suffolk, May 3, 1863, and died after returning home. Letter 5/5/63.

Dixon, David P. - Age, 21 years. Enlisted, September 16, 1861 at Delhi, to serve three years; mustered in as private, October 21, 1861; promoted first sergeant, no date; discharged October 21, 1864. Born New York City. Letters 5/29/62, 2/3/63, 2/15/63, 12/3/63 and 1/16/64.

Dougherty, John - Age, 23 years. Enlisted, September 16, 1861 at Delhi, to serve three years; mustered in as private, October 21, 1861; discharged October 30, 1864. Also borne as Doherty. Born Walton, NY.

Drake, David M. - Age, 31 years. Enlisted, September 16, 1861 at Delhi, to serve three years; mustered in as corporal, November 6, 1861; died October 20, 1862 at Harper's Ferry, VA., of Typhoid Fever.

Drummond, William - Age, 24 years. Enlisted, September 16, 1861 at Delhi, to serve three years; mustered in as private, October 21, 1861; discharged October 24, 1864. Born Delhi, NY. Letters 1/30/64

and 7/16/64.

Dyer, Reuben[46] - Age, 23 years. Enlisted, September 16, 1861 at Delhi, to serve three years; mustered in as private, October 21, 1861; re-enlisted as veteran, January 4, 1864; promoted sergeant, June 1, 1865; mustered out with company August 3, 1865 at Richmond, VA; also borne as Dyre. He was a pensioner. Letter 1/10/64.

England, Theophilus L. - Age, 24 years. Enrolled, September 16, 1861 at Delhi, to serve three years; mustered in as captain November 13, 1861; as lieutenant colonel, February 18, 1863; killed in action June 16, 1864, before Petersburg, VA; also borne as T. F. England. Commissioned captain, December 18, 1861 with rank from October 31, 1861, original; lieutenant colonel, March 23, 1863, with rank from February 17, 1863, vice N. Coryell resigned. Letters 12/5/61, 12/28/61, 6/2/62 and 8/17/62, 8/27/62, 2/15/63, 3/2/63, 4/20/63, 4/27/63, and 3/25/64.

Epes, Wesley - Age, 19 years. Enlisted, September 16, 1861 at Delhi, to serve three years; mustered in as private, October 25, 1861; died, November 25, 1861, at Elmira, NY; also borne as John W. Epps. Surgeon's report says died of pneumonia as a complication of measles. Letters 11/28/61 and 12/28/61.

Epps, Henry W. - Age, 26 years. Enlisted, September 16, 1861 at Delhi, to serve three years; mustered in as sergeant, December 4, 1861; promoted second lieutenant June 27, 1862; first lieutenant August 1, 1863; captured in action September 29, 1864, at Chaffin's Farm, VA; paroled March 1, 1865; mustered in as captain, Co. K, June 13, 1865; mustered out with company August 3, 1865 at Richmond, VA; also borne as Epes and Eppes; prior service in Indian war in Oregon. Commissioned second lieutenant August 28, 1862, vice J. S. Ronk, resigned, with rank from June 27, 1862; first lieutenant July 23, 1863, with rank from December 27, 1862, vice R.P. Cormack promoted; captain, May 31, 1865, with rank from May 18, 1865, vice F. W. Tremain, promoted. Born in Delaware County, NY. Letters 5/5/63 and 7/16/64.

---

[46] R. Dyer was African American. He served and fought in a White regiment at a time when most Blacks were rejected by the military. Personal communication, used with permission.

Feibig, Charles - Age, 40 years. Enlisted, September 16, 1861 at Delhi, to serve three years; mustered in as sergeant, October 21, 1861; discharged October 31, 1864. Letters 5/9/62 and 4/27/63.

Flowers, Artemas D. - Age, 24 years. Enlisted, September 16, 1861 at Delhi, to serve three years; mustered in as private, October 21, 1861; died February 2, 1863 at Falmouth, VA, of chronic diarrhea; also borne as Artimus D.

Flowers, Charles N. - Age, 26 years. Enlisted, September 16, 1861 at Delhi, to serve three years; mustered in as private, October 21, 1861; died, September 1, 1864, at Point of Rocks, MD, of chronic diarrhea; also borne as Charles W.

Flowers, Henry - Age, 18 years. Enlisted, September 16, 1861 at Delhi, to serve three years; mustered in as private, November 15, 1861; discharged for disability October 3, 1863.

Gaston, Anderson - Age, 40 years. Enlisted, September 16, 1861 at Delhi, to serve three years; mustered in as private November 1, 1861; discharged October 30, 1864. Also borne as Gorton. Born Charlestown, Mass. Letter 1/30/64.

Gilbert, William J. - Age, 18 years. Enlisted, September 16, 1861 at Delhi, to serve three years; mustered in as musician, December 4, 1861; discharged, December 3, 1864. Born Delhi, NY.

Graham, Charles - Age, 25 years. Enlisted, September 16, 1861, at Delhi, to serve three years; mustered in as corporal, Co. I, October 21, 1861; promoted sergeant, no date; discharged October 21, 1864. Other source says wounded before Petersburgh, Va. Born Franklin Couny, NY.

Gray, George B. - Age, 21 years. Enlisted, September 16, 1861 at Delhi, to serve three years; mustered in as private October 21, 1861; discharged October 21, 1864; also borne as Grey. Born Walton, NY. Letter 9/28/62.

Gregory, Calvin - Age, 40 years. Enlisted, September 16, 1861, at Delhi, to serve three years; mustered in as corporal, Co. I, October 25, 1861; discharged for disability, February 16, 1863. Born in Canada.

Gross, Harmon - Age, 23 years. Enlisted, September 16, 1861 at Delhi, to serve three years; mustered in as private, October 21, 1861; deserted, August 6, 1864 at Alexandria, VA; also borne as Heman.

Halstead, William C. - Age, 22 years. Enlisted, September 16, 1861 at Delhi, to serve three years; mustered in as private October 21, 1861; died, April 20, 1862, at Roanoke Is., NC, of Typhoid Fever; also borne as Holstead. Letters 11/5/61, 2/6/62, 3/13/62, 3/31/62, 4/62, 4/8/62, 4/21/62, 4/22/62, 5/9/62, 5/22/62, and 3/25/64.

Harvey, Charles E. - Age, 29 years. Enlisted at Middlefield, to serve three years, and mustered in as private, Co. I, January 28, 1864; no further record.

Harder, Benjamin - Age, 43 years. Enlisted, September 16, 1861 at Delhi, to serve three years; mustered in as private October 21, 1861; discharged for disability, December 10, 1862.

Havens, Alonzo - Age, 22 years. Enlisted, September 16, 1861 at Delhi, to serve three years; mustered in as private, December 4, 1861; deserted, December 5, 1861, at Elmira, NY.

Henderson, Harvey - Age, 21 years. Enlisted, September 16, 1861 at Delhi, to serve three years; mustered in as private, October 21, 1861; promoted corporal, August 9, 1862; sergeant December 29, 1863; captured September 23, 1864; pardoned, no date; mustered out with company, August 3, 1865, at Richmond, VA. Another source says discharged April, 1865. Born Delaware County, NY.

Hine, Burton - Age, 19 years. Enlisted, September 16, 1861 at Delhi, to serve three years; mustered in as private October 21, 1861; promoted corporal, February 25, 1863; discharged, October 21, 1864; prior service in 27th Militia. Born in Meredith, NY.

Hitchcock, George W. - Age, 18 years. Enlisted, September 16, 1861 at Delhi, to serve three years; mustered in as private, October 31, 1861; promoted corporal, no date; re-enlisted as veteran, January 14, 1864; promoted sergeant, July 1, 1865; quartermaster sergeant, July 20, 1865; mustered out with regiment, August 3, 1865, at Richmond, VA. Letter 12/28/62.

Hitchcock, William - Age, 39 years. Enlisted, September 16, 1861 at

Delhi, to serve three years; mustered in as corporal, November 15, 1861; promoted sergeant, no date; transferred to Veteran Reserve Corps, July 1, 1863. Discharged in November of 1864 as a sergeant in the 18th. Born in Delaware County, NY.

Houck, George W. - Age, 21 years. Enlisted, September 16, 1861 at Delhi, to serve three years; mustered in as private, December 4, 1861; discharged, December 6, 1864; also borne as Honck

Hoyt, Sherman -Age, 20 years. Enlisted, September 16, 1861 at Delhi, to serve three years; mustered in as private, October 21, 1861; killed in action, August 28, 1862, at Falmouth, VA; also borne as Sherman S. Hoys. The surgeon's report states that he died while guarding a railroad bridge on the Potomac, and fell asleep on the track.

Hughes, Patrick - Age, 23 years. Enlisted, September 16, 1861 at Delhi, to serve three years; mustered in as private, October 21, 1861; discharged for disability, February 11, 1863. Letter 9/28/62.

Jacobs, Ira D. - Age, 24 years. Enlisted, November 6, 1861 at Delhi, to serve three years; mustered in as corporal, November 29, 1861; promoted first sergeant, no date; died, August 19, 1863 at Folly Island, SC, of dysentery. Commissioned, not mustered, second lieutenant, July 23, 1863 with rank from December 27, 1862, vice H. H. Epps promoted. Letters 5/22/62, 7/3/62, 9/19/63, and 10/24/63.

Johnson, James - Age, 37 years. Enlisted, September 16, 1861 at Delhi, to serve three years; mustered in as private, Co. I, October 21, 1861; discharged for disability Nov. 9, 1863.

Johnson, James - Age, 43 years. Enlisted, January 4, 1864, at Sheldrake, to serve three years; mustered in as private, Co. I, January 5, 1864; captured, no date; died in confederate prison, September 3, 1864, at Andersonville, Ga.

Jones, Addison - Age, 23 years. Enlisted, October 28, 1861, at Delhi to serve three years; mustered in as private, Co. I, November 1, 1861; discharged October 30, 1864.

Jones, Albert W. - Age, 26 years. Enlisted, September 16, 1861 at Delhi, to serve three years; mustered in as private, Co. I, October 31,

1861; killed before Petersburgh, Va, July 13, 1864. The surgeon's report says killed instantly when struck in the chest by a Whitworth shell, which laid open the entire chest cavity. Letter 7/16/64.

Jones, Alexis - Age, 31 years. Enlisted, September 16, 1861 at Delhi, to serve three years; mustered in as corporal, Co. I, November 5, 1861; wounded in action in the left arm September 17, 1862 at Antietam; promoted sergeant December 1, 1863; wounded and captured in action October 29, 1864 at Seven Pines, Va; paroled February 5, 1865; discharged March 9, 1865. Born in Rhode Island, he enlisted from Masonville in 1861. After he was wounded he was taken to Richmond, where he had his right arm amputated at the shoulder, it having been damaged too severely by the ball. Letter 9/28/62

Keator, M. Sands - Age, 22 years. Enlisted, September 16, 1861, at Delhi, to serve three years; mustered in as private, Co. I, October 21, 1861; promoted corporal, no date; discharged for disability, January 29, 1862; also borne as Sands M.

Kniskern, James E. - Age, 23 years. Enlisted, September 16, 1861, at Delhi, to serve three years; mustered in as private, Co. I, October 21, 1861; discharged October 21, 1864; also borne as Kniskem and Knisken. Born Blenheim, NY.

Kniskern, Levi J. - Age, 19 years. Enlisted, September 16, 1861, at Delhi, to serve three years; mustered in as private, Co. I, October 31, 1861; discharged, October 21, 1864; also borne as Kniskem and Knisken. Born in Schoharie County, NY.

Law, Nathaniel A. - Age, 22 years. Enlisted, September 16, 1861, at Delhi, to serve three years; mustered in as private, Co. I, February, 1862; discharged for disability, October 11, 1862. Letter 9/28/62.

Law, William S. - Age, 21 years. Enlisted, September 16, 1861, at Delhi, to serve three years; mustered in as private, Co. I, October 21, 1861; captured, June 12, 1864 at Cold Harbor, Va; paroled, April 21, 1865; discharged, June 29, 1865, at New York City. Letter 1/30/64.

Lee, Daniel - Age, 24 years. Enlisted, September 16, 1861, at Delhi, to serve three years; mustered in as sergeant, Co. I, October 21, 1861; returned to ranks, no date; promoted corporal, December 29, 1863;

mustered out with company, August 3, 1865 at Richmond, Va. Also listed as David Lee. Born in Delaware County, NY. Letters 3/31/62, 4/8/62, 12/2/62, 1/19/63, 6/21/63, and 10/6/64.

Little, James - Age, 21 years. Enlisted, September 16, 1861, at Delhi, to serve three years; mustered in as private, Co. I, October 21, 1861; discharged, October 21, 1864. Letter 5/21/64 indicates he was wounded. Born in Delhi, NY.

Mains, Daniel - Age, 28 years. Enlisted, September 16, 1861, at Delhi, to serve three years; mustered in as private, Co. I, October 21, 1861; promoted corporal, October 28, 1863; captured in action, September 29, 1864, at Chaffin's Farm, Va.; paroled, no date; mustered out with company, August 3, 1865, at Richmond, Va. Born in Scotland. Letters 7/16/64 and 7/31/64, latter of which reports wounding in the shoulder in July of 1864.

Mason, Augustus - Age, 19 years. Enlisted, September 16, 1861, at Delhi, to serve three years; mustered in as private, Co. I, November 19, 1861; died, August 18, 1862, at Roanoke Island, NC., of Typhoid Fever.

Mitchell, McCombs - Age, 42 years. Enlisted, November 10, 1861, at Delhi, to serve three years; mustered in as private, Co. I, November 21, 1861; discharged for disability, August 13, 1863; also borne as Mitchell McCombs. Another source says he died in hospital.

Munn, John A. - Age, 22 years. Enlisted, September 16, 1861, at Delhi, to serve three years; mustered in as private, Co. I, October 21, 1861; discharged October 21, 1864. Another source says taken prisoner.

Murphy, Isaiah - Age, 18 years. Enlisted, September 16, 1861, at Delhi, to serve three years; mustered in as private, Co. I, October 21, 1861; died, July 7, 1862, at Washington, DC., of pneumonia. Also called Isaac.

Newton, Nathan A. - Age, 28 years. Enrolled, August 1, 1861, at Binghamton, to serve three years; mustered in as first lieutenant, Co. B, September 10, 1861; as captain, Co. I, February 18, 1863; discharged October 29, 1864; also borne as Nathan L. Commissioned first lieutenant, December 18, 1861, with rank from August 31, 1861, original; captain, March 23, 1863 with rank from February 17, 1863, vice T.L. England promoted.

O'Donnell, Jeremiah - Age, 26 years. Enlisted, September 16, 1861, at Delhi, to serve three years; mustered in as first sergeant, Co. I, October 21, 1861; returned to ranks, no date; discharged, no date. Letters 3/15/62, 2/10/63, 2/15/63,

Olmstead, Sheldon T. - Age, 19. Enlisted, September 16, 1861, at Delhi, to serve three years; mustered in as private, Co. I, November 6, 1861; transferred to Second U.S. Cavalry in December 1862; also borne as Sheldon P. Letter 9/28/62.

Patterson, John H. - Age, 22 years. Enlisted, September 16, 1861, at Delhi, to serve three years; mustered in as private, Co. I, October 21, 1861; discharged, October 21, 1864.

Patterson, Smith B. - Age, 27 years. Enlisted, September 16, 1861, at Delhi, to serve three years; mustered in as private, Co. I, November 21, 1861; discharged, November 19, 1864. Born, Bloomville, NY.

Pine, John D. - Age, 20 years. Enlisted, November 13, 1861, at Delhi, to serve three years; mustered in as private, Co. I, November 15, 1861; transferred to Veteran Reserve Corps, July 1, 1863. Discharged in November of 1864 from Co. C of 3 NY

Purdy, Darius - Age, 26 years. Enlisted, September 16, 1861, at Delhi, to serve three years; mustered in as private, Co. I, October 21, 1861; deserted, August 28, 1862, at Newport News, Va.; also borne as Davis Purdy.

Reed, Chauncey J. - Age, 24 years. Enrolled, October 1, 1861, at Binghamton, to serve three years; mustered in as private, Co. B., October 21, 1861; as second lieutenant, December 5, 1861; discharged, October 5, 1862; again enrolled and mustered in as private, Co. I, January 4, 1864; promoted sergeant, and sergeant-major, no dates; mustered in as first lieutenant, Co. E., February 18, 1865; mustered out with company, August 3, 1865, at Richmond, Va.; also borne as Chauncey P. Reid and Read.

Reynolds, Gaine - Age, 19 years. Enlisted, March 1, 1864, at Kortright, to serve three years; mustered in as private, Co. I, April 7,

1864; died, February 13, 1865 at Deep Bottom, Va.; also borne as Gaivns H.

Rivenbury, William - Age, 20 years. Enlisted, November 6, 1861, at Delhi, to serve three years; mustered in as private, Co. I, November 18, 1861; re-enlisted as veteran, December 27, 1863; mustered out with company, August 3, 1865, at Richmond, Va.; also borne as William K. and Rivenbergh and Revinbury. Other information says wounded before Petersburgh, Va. Born in Roxbury, NY. Letters 1/10/64 and 7/16/64.

Robinson, William A. - Age, 29 years. Enlisted, September 16, 1861, at Delhi, to serve three years; mustered in as corporal, Co. I, October 21, 1861; returned to ranks and appointed wagoner, no dates; discharged, October 21, 1864. Author of the letters.

Ronk, Julius S. - Age, 21 years. Enrolled, October 25, 1861, at Binghamton, to serve three years; mustered in as second lieutenant, Co. I, December 5, 1861; discharged, July 15, 1862; also borne as Brooks, Rank and Rook. Commissioned second lt., December 18, 1861, with rank from December 4, 1861, original. Letter 12/28/61

Schuff, Philip - Age, 28 years. Enlisted, September 16, 1861, at Delhi, to serve three years; mustered in as private, Co. I, October 25, 1861; died, July 28, 1862, at Norfolk, Va., of Typhoid Fever; also borne as Philip Scheff.

Scott, William - Age, 23 years. Enlisted at Delhi, to serve three years, and mustered in as private, Co. I, January 4, 1864; mustered out with company, August 3, 1865, at Richmond, Va.; veteran.

Seymour, Daniel E. - Age, 24 years. Enlisted, September 16, 1861, at Delhi, to serve three years; mustered in as private, Co. I, October 21, 1861; discharged, October 21, 1864; also borne as Seemer. Letter 9/28/62.

Shelaman, Philander - Age, 23 years. Enlisted, September 16, 1861, at Delhi, to serve three years; mustered in as private, Co. I, October 21, 1861; discharged, October 21, 1864.

Silliman, Charles F. - Age, 21 years. Enlisted, September 16, 1861, at Delhi, to serve three years; mustered in as private, Co. I,

November 6, 1861; transferred to Veteran Reserve Corps, July 1, 1863; also borne as Selliman. Discharged as sergeant Co. E of 6th NY. Born in Delaware Co. Letter, 1/30/64.

Simmons, James - Age, 18 years. Enlisted, September 16, 1861, at Delhi, to serve three years; mustered in as private, Co. I, October 21, 1861; re-enlisted as veteran, January 14, 1864; mustered out with company, August 3, 1865, at Richmond, Va. Letter 4/20/63.

Southwick, Benjamin - Age, 22 years. Enlisted, March 22, 1864, at Otego, to serve three years; mustered in as private, Co. I, March 23, 1864. No further record.

Stilson, Nathan - Age, 35 years. Enlisted, September 16, 1861, at Delhi, to serve three years; mustered in as wagoner, Co. I, November 5, 1861; discharged for disability, August 13, 1862. Letter 8/27/62.

Stott, George W. - Age, 30 years. Enlisted, December 1, 1861, at Delhi, to serve three years; mustered in as private, Co. I, December 4, 1861; re-enlisted as veteran, January 5, 1864; discharged, December 4, 1864; also borne as Slott, and William G. Letters 1/10/64 and 1/30/64.

Sullivan, John W. - Age, 32 years. Enlisted, September 16, 1861, at Delhi, to serve three years; mustered in as musician, Co. I, October 21, 1861; deserted, August 28, 1862, at Newport News, Va.

Thomas, David - Age, 18 years. Enlisted, October 3, 1861, at Delhi, to serve three years; mustered in as private, Co. I, November 6, 1861; absent, missing in action, since October 27, 1864, and at muster-out of company. Another source says killed at Chaffin's Farm, Va. October 21, 1864.

Thompson, John - Age, 20 years. Enlisted, September 16, 1861, at Delhi, to serve three years; mustered in as private, Co. I, October 21, 1861; discharged October 21, 1864. Born in Glasco, Scotland. Letter 5/5/63 indicates wounded at Suffolk, Va.

Thompson, Thomas E. - Age, 21 years. Enlisted, October 31, 1861, at Delhi, to serve three years; mustered in as private, Co. I, November 21, 1861; promoted corporal in February, 1864; wounded, no date; absent, in hospital, since May 20, 1864, and at muster out of company. Another source says wounded at Battle of Weir Bottom Church, Va., on June 16, 1864. Letter 5/21/64.

Van Slyck, Albert - Age, 19 years. Enlisted, September 16, 1861, at Delhi, to serve three years; mustered in as private, Co. I, October 21, 1861; discharged for disability, February 8, 1864; also borne as Van Slyk.

White, John J. - Age, 19 years. Enlisted, September 16, 1861, at Delhi, to serve three years; mustered in as private, Co. I, October 21, 1861; discharged, October 21, 1864. Letter 9/28/62 says wounded at Antietam, Md., also letter 4/3/64.

Wight, James - Age, 22 years. Enlisted, September 16, 1861, at Delhi, to serve three years; mustered in as private, Co. I, October 21, 1861; re-enlisted as veteran, January 5, 1864; mustered out with company, August 3, 1865, at Richmond, Va. Born in Delhi, NY. Letters 1/10/64, 1/30/64, 2/13/64.

Wood, Stephen E. - Age, 23 years. Enlisted, September 16, 1861, at Delhi, to serve three years; mustered in as private, Co. I, October 21, 1861; discharged, December 20, 1864. Letter 9/28/62 says wounded at Antietam, Md.

Zee, Robert - Age, 19 years. Enlisted, September 16, 1861, at Delhi, to serve three years; mustered in as private, Co. I, October 21, 1861; deserted, October 29, 1862, at Orlean, Va.; also borne as Zeh. Letters 12/12/61, 4/8/62, 9/28/62, and 10/24/63.

Appendix B - Regimental Staff Officers

- Colonel -

Harrison S. Fairchild. See page 145.

- Lieutenant Colonels -

Jacob B. Robie. Age, 52 years. Enrolled at Binghamton, to serve three years, and mustered in as Lt. Col., December 5, 1861; discharged October 4, 1862. Prior service in New York Militia.

Nathan Coryell. Age, 44 years. Enrolled, August 5, 1861, at Havana, to serve three years; mustered in as captain, Co. A, December 4, 1861; as Lt. Col., October 4, 1862; discharged, February 17, 1863, at Newport News, Va; also borne as N. A. Coryell.

Theophilus L. England. See page 150.

Wellington M. Lewis. Age, 20 years. Enrolled, October 11, 1861, at Binghamton, to serve three years; mustered in as first lieutenant, Co. H, December 4, 1861; captain, November 27, 1862; major, May 10, 1864; lt. col., October 13, 1864; wounded in action, October 27, 1864 at Fair Oaks, Va.; discharged for disability from wounds, May 15, 1865; also borne as H. M. Lewis.

Henry C. Roome. Age, 23 years. Enrolled, September 23, 1861, at Oxford, to serve three years; mustered in as second lieutenant, Co. E, December 4, 1861; captain, October 15, 1862; captured in action, September 29, 1864, at Chaffin's Farm, Va.; paroled in March of 1865; discharged August 16, 1865 at Richmond, Va.; also borne as Broome, Roame and Roone.

- Majors -

Daniel T. Everts. Age, 29 years. Enrolled at Elmira, to serve three years, adn mustered in as major, December 4, 1861; discharged for disability, March 2, 1864; also borne as Everetts.

Jardine, Edward. See page 122. (Is not listed in Phisterer's)

Wellington Lewis. See above, this page.

Frank W. Tremain. Age, 18 years. Enrolled, October 16, 1861, at Lanesboro, Pa., to serve three years; mustered in as second lieutenant, Co. K, December 5, 1861; as first lt., March 21, 1863; captain, July 13, 1864; major, March 14, 1865; killed in action, April 2, 1865, at Fort Gregg, Va.; also borne as Tremaine.

- Adjutant -

John E. Shepard. Age, 26 years. Enrolled at Waverly, to serve three years; mustered in as first lieutenant and adjutant, December 5, 1861; mustered out, December 4, 1864; also borne as Shephard.

- Quartermasters -

Cornelius H. Webster. Age, 42 years. Enrolled at Elmira, to serve three years, and mustered in as first lieutenant and quartermaster, December 4, 1861; discharged, December 30, 1863;

Charles H. Amsbry. Age, 22 years. Enrolled, September 24, 1861, at Binghamton, to serve three years; mustered in as sergeant, Co. H., October 14, 1861; as second lt. December 31, 1862; first lt. and quartermaster, December 31, 1863; captain, Co. A, June 1, 1865; mustered out with company, August 3, 1865, at Richmond, Va., also borne as Amsbury and Armsby.

- Surgeon -

Truman H. Squire. Age, 38 years. Enrolled at Elmira, to serve three years, and mustered in as surgeon, November 29, 1861; mustered out, December 4, 1864; again enrolled, and mustered in as surgeon, January 9, 1865; discharged, May 19, 1865, at Richmond, Va.; also borne as Squares.

- Assistant Surgeons -

William A. Smith. Age, 41 years. Enrolled at Elmira, to serve three years, and mustered in as assistant surgeon, December 4, 1861; promoted to surgeon in One Hundred and Third Infantry, December 8, 1862.

James J. Allen. Age, 34 years. Enrolled, November 16, 1861, at

Yorkshire, to serve three years; mustered in as private, Co. F, November 18, 1861; promoted hospital steward, December 1, 1861; mustered in as assistant surgeon, August 28, 1862; mustered out November 20, 1864.

M. Eugene Shaw. Enrolled, December 10, 1862, at Albany, to serve three years; mustered in as assistant surgeon, January 30, 1863; discharged, October 11, 1863.

- Chaplains -

Nathaniel E. Pierson. Age, 47 years. Enrolled at Elmira, to serve three years, and mustered in as chaplain, December 5, 1861; discharged, November 23, 1862, at Falmouth, Va. Also borne as Peirreson.

Willard Richardson. Age, 48 years. Enrolled, February 23, 1864, at Fort Monroe, Va., to serve three years; mustered in as chaplain, May 7, 1864; discharged, March 16, 1865.

Appendix C - Rosters of Men in Eighty Ninth NY Volunteer Infantry other than Company I

Company A

Adams, Henry C.

Bacon, William A.
Baker, Almon
Brady, James T.
Burke, Benjamin H.

Cahill, William A.
Carpenter, Birdsall
Carson, George W.
Clanharty, Edgar W.
Coleman, Coe R.
Compton, William A.
Coryell, Charles A.
Cramer, John D.
Creegan, Jeffery
Curry, Edwin B.

Dean, Douglass
Demund, Leroy
Doane, Joseph S.
Dominick, John W.
Dudlew, George W.

Earnest, Clinton D.
Elyea, Charles

Feeley, Martin
Forrest, Nathaniel I.
Francisco, Henry R.

Geelard, John
Gordon, William H.

Hannon, Peter
Harris, Ebben
Havencamp, Oliver P.

Agney, Irving

Baker, Adolph
Bickal, Darius
Brown, Solomon
Burnett, Albert N.

Cannon, Robert
Carpenter, John M.
Cary, Archibald
Clark, Alanson
Colton, Charles
Cormack, Robert P.
Coryell, Nathan
Crandall, William
Creque, Abram M.

Dean, Wilson
Dibble, Ira
Dolan, Michael
Donahue, John
Dumas, David H.

Egbert, Charles

Folmsbee, George R.
Fowler, Charles O.

Gilbert, Albert
Guiney, Daniel

Harris, Averill
Harris, George
Hillinger, John

Holden, James
Houck, Mentiaville S.
Hulien, Frank

Jessop, John H.

Kelley, Andrew
Kelly, Seneca
Kinsick, Herman
Knapp, David M.
Kunz, Charles

Lambert, Decatur
Latourno, Joseph
Lee, James
Lewis, Isaiah
Linsenhoff, Rudolph
Loutz, Adam
Lybolt, Albert

Manning, James E.
Marshall, George E.
Martin, John
Mason, Mitchell
Maxwell, Albert
McGrimpsey, William
McLaughlin, Charles
Merritt, Emory
Miller, William H.

Newark, Frederick
Northrup, Sevellon W.

O'Brien, John

Patrick, Aaron S.
Peck, John W.
Pratt, Edward N.
Proper, Gilbert

Quackenbush, John

Horton, Austin
Hughes, George
Hunt, Eben

Julien, Theopolis

Kellogg, Edwin S.
Kiel, Fredrick
Kirtland, John C.
Knapp, George H.

Lane, Thaddeus W.
Lawrence, Stephen D.
Letts, Delos
Lindrob, John
Loomis, Charles
Lovell, Salmon S.

Manning, Silas
Marshall, James E.
Martin, Nathan
Mathews, Frederick A.
Maxwell, John
McKune, Gilbert E.
Merrick, William H.
Miller, Jacob
Myre, John

Nixon, William I.

Owen, Charles

Patzack, Charles
Pixley, John W.
Pratt, Henry

Rima, Henry
Rossiter, Edward A.
Rowley, Henry E.

Rose, Jacob. H.
Rosten, Frederick

Sarsefield, Thomas
Simmons, Alfred
Smith, Jacob
Smith, Silas M. N.
Solomon, Solomon A.
Spades, John
Stay, Oliver
Stinefield, Philipp
Strong, Munson
Sullivan, Patrick
Swallow, Isaac W.

Shephard, William A.
Sims, Samuel L.
Smith, Orcelas C.
Smith, William B.
Soule, Alfred W.
Specht, Joseph
Stilwell, Schuyler
Stone, Peter
Strubell, George
Sullivan, Patrick

Tailby, John
Taylor, Israel S.
Thomas, Edward
Thurtston, William

Tailby, William Jr.
Tesck, Henry
Thomson, George W.
Turner, Albert H.

VanBuskirk, Dermont
Varian, Isaac B.

VanGelder, William S.
Vosburgh, Francis S.

Wasson, John
Waterfield, Dewitt
Wesley, John
Whitehead, William
Wicks, Benjamin
Williams, Mordicia

Wasson, Samuel
Weed, Eliphalet Jr.
Whitehead, Alonzo B.
Wick, William A.
William, Henry L.
Wolvarton, Reading

Yadder, John

Company B

Anson, Leanord

Badger, Byron N.
Baker, George C.
Beardsley, John W.
Birley, William

Baker, Chauncey
Bartlett, Lewis Chester
Berger, Jacob
Bishop, Edward B.

Bolles, Stephen H.
Brown, Andrew J.
Burr, James S.
Busby, James E.

Bovee, Joseph
Brown, Frederick
Burt, Albert C.

Cafferty, Edward M.
Cameron, Jehiel
Carhart, George W.
Cassidy, John
Clyde, Alfred
Cook, Sherman N.
Crane, Robert W.
Curtis, Azor M.

Cagdin, Stephen
Campbell, Charles L.
Cash, Uriah W.
Cluen, John
Collan, Thomas
Corry, Nelson
Crumb, Samuel D.

Davis, Edson A.
Denison, Daniel
Duel, Seneca
Durfee, Thomas

Delano, Martin
Downs, Richard
Durand, David C.

Evans, William E.

Fischer, William C.

Francisco, Reed F.

Garrett, James
Gray, Arthur O.
Groody, Thomas

Gould, Hiram D.
Groody, James
Grove, George A.

Hall, William H.
Harris, David
Hunt, John P.

Hamilton, William
Hazley, James

Kay, John

Kelly, Benjamin

Landon, Hiram D.
Lincoln, David

Leech, Benjamin F.

Mallan, James
Manderville, John F.
Mason, Fletcher
Munn, John W.

Mallon, John
Mann, Jerry
Maunskoff, John

Needrick, Adam

Northrup, Frank E.

O'Clary, Francis

O'Connor, James

Patterson, David A.
Pierson, Lewis M.
Portsher, Jacob
Pratt, Friend

Pierce, Edward M.
Pithie, Charles
Powers, William T.

Ranny, Oliver
Rockwell, John W.

Reed, Chauncey, J.
Rulifson, John W.

Soriver, Ira
Spahn, John
Stringham, George W.

Smith, Richard
Stringham, Charles
Sweet, John H.

Towner, Ernest F.

VanAuken, Jacob
Vandervort, Martin

Vanderburgh, Henry W.

Waldron, Jacob W.
Williams, Charles H.

Watrus, Marvin

Company C

Andrus, Elisha B.

Baker, Thomas L.
Bennett, Richard S.
Bingham, Albert M.
Boughton, William A.
Burt, Charles W.

Beers, William L.
Biggs, William M
Bischoff, William
Brady, Warren
Burt, Tyrell

Campbell, Andrew J.
Chamberlain, William N.
Collins, John
Cook, Aaron
Craft, Benjamin

Centre, Lucius
Cole, Parker
Collsen, Andrew J.
Copeland, John

Davenport, John J.
Dunn, John

Deiffinbucher, Norman
Dusenbury, William

Eddy, William T.
Faxen, William H.
Forbes, John

Gardner, Avery

Harknies, George
Hart, Edward F.
Henry, Charles
Humfrey, Willis B.

Johnson, John C.

Keeney, Ansel F.

Lands, Benjamin F.

Mann, John
McCarthy, John
Miner, Eliakim

Neff, Lewis A.

Overton, Elsbury

Peck, Charles F.
Pettibone, Levi
Poppino, Franklin

Reany, Ansel F.

Sandford, Daniel T.
Shuart, Alanson, K.
Spencer, George

Thatcher, Joseph F.
Traver, Lucius
Truman, John P.

VanAntwerp, Adelbert S.

Eldridge, Chauncey P.

Foote, Giles

Harrington, Charles H.
Hathorn, John L.
Hill, William Jr.
Humphrey, George H.

Jones, Samuel

Kettle, John B.

Leonard, Zebina A.

Marsh, David H.
McHenry, Joseph

Nichols, Samuel

Peck, Chillion
Phelps, Jessie

Rulapaugh, Nicholas

Scott, Charles
Simmons, Alpheus S.

Townsend, Homer N.
Truman, John A. R. P.
Tweedey, Joseph V.

VanAntwerp, Irving L.

VanBuren, Dean
Walker, John D.
Webster, Eugene
Williams, John P.

VanDerbelt, Marcus H.
Ward, Jeremiah
Wilcox, Cuyler F.
Wilson, Lanora

Company D

Alden, Edwin

Ambrose, Richard

Baker, Alonzo D.
Beck, John
Boran, Charles
Briggs, Calvin
Brown, Peter
Buckley, Michael

Baker, William
Boland, Patrick
Brady, John
Brooks, John
Bruton, Patrick

Caesar, William
Casey, Barney
Clements, John
Cooney, William
Corrigan, James
Cowles, Chandler

Cameron, Daniel
Clark, William
Conroy, Terence
Cooper, Owen
Cottar, John
Cush, Michael

Daley, Francis
Delaney, Daniel P.
Devereux, Mathew
Dobie, William
Donovan, Daniel
Doyle, John
Dwyer, William

Davis, George
Demarest, John
Dobie, George
Donnely, James
Dowley, William
Durand, Eugene

Eddy, Martin
Essler, John

Egan, Michael
Evridge, Albert

Farnsworth, William
Fitzgibbons, Patrick
Forbes, David

Farrall, John
Flannagan, Thomas

Gammell, David
Gillespie, Francis

Garrotty, Thomas
Green, Peter H.

Griffin, William
Gwynne, Sidney George

Griffiths, Edward

Hadley, Charles
Hare, Thomas
Higgins, John
Hughs, Peter W.

Hardgrove, Lawrence
Hawes, Daniel
House, Frederick

Jackson, John

Jordan, John A.

Keefe, John
Kelly, Dennis
Kendelen, Charles
Kirby, Peter

Keelcher, Cornelius
Kelly, William
Kennedy, Robert
Kirch, John

Lawless, Edward W.
Leahy, James
Lefebore, Jean Louis

Lawless, John
Ledwith, Edmund
Lumsden, Augustus G.

Lyons, John

Machurell, Harvey
Mathews, Frank
McCarthy, Thomas
McConnell, William
McGuire, George
McKee, George
McMullen, William
Miller, Charles
Miller, John
Molloy, John
Morrison, Alexander
Morrisey, John
Munn, James M.
Myers, Henry

Martin, David D.
McBrien, Henry
McChurch, Harvey
McDonald, William
McKay, Samuel H.
McKinley, William
McNichols, Michael
Miller, James
Mitchell, James
Morgan, John
Morrison, Joseph
Mulligan, John
Murphy, Felix

Nelligan, Simon

O'Brien, Michael

O'Neil, James

Passage, Eugene
Pelham, Levi A.

Patterson, William
Perkins, Silas A.

Pierve, Henry
Pithie, David
Plopper, Madison H.

Pierson, Peter H.
Platt, William
Pringle, Albert

Quinn, John

Ramsey, David
Read, Patrick
Reilly, Michael
Ryan, James

Raw, George E.
Reierdon, Daniel
Remington, Jeremiah
Ryan, Patrick

Scott, James
Slyter, George
Smith, John
Spock, Christian
Steams, Stacey A.
Sullivan, Cornelius

Shannon, Joseph
Smith, Edward H.
Sommers, Louis
Stafford, John
Storrs, Thomas
Sullivan, Michael

Thomson, George
Thousand, John
Tracey, Henry

Thomson, Jacob C.
Titus, Charles F.

Valsh, Thomas

Wagner, George
Warner, Asahel
Whelan, John
Winters, William G.

Wald, John
Welsh, Thomas
Winn, John
Wood, Charles

Company E

Albert, Conrad

Ames, Marsene B.

Bailey, George C.
Ball, Charles
Barber, Thomas A.
Barr, Alonzo
Belden, Elias M.
Boardman, James
Boyd, Rufus
Burlingam, Martin A.

Balcomb, Samuel
Ballou, George
Barnes, Franklin C.
Barrows, Truman
Benedict, Jerome
Bowers, Gilbert
Brown, William P.
Burnside, George M.

Butler, William W.
Button, Henry A.

Cady, George
Carr, George H.
Church, Ransom E.
Clinton, William Y., Jr.
Crandall, Emerson C.
Crawford, Lewis
Cunningham, Wilner

Dailey, David P.
Davis, Harvey D.
Dixon, Simeon
Duffy, Richard

Edwards, Orville A.
Evans, Mordica

Figari, John H.
Figari, Oscar M.
Foster, Ralph L.

Guernsey, William B.

Hammond, Henry
Harris, Benjamin E.
Harris, William H.
Harvey, Rodney A.
Holdridge, Warden
Hopkins, Albert
Huntley, Lewis

Isbell, Elmer

Jacobs, Israel P.
Johnson, George H.

Lewis, Jay
Lorio, Joseph

Butler, William W.

Carpenter, Nemihiah
Chamberlain, Samuel W.
Clinton, Jesse B.
Corker, Joseph
Cranell, Daniel
Crumb, David H.

Davenport, Frederick
Dibble, Lyman
Doyle, Henry C.

Edwards, Rufus
Everson, Charles S.

Figari, John T.
Foster, Orville L.
Fowler, Orin P.

Harriott, Thomas B.
Harris, Richard G.
Hart, Clinton
Holdridge, Amos B.
Holdridge, Wiley P.
Hulbert, Ephraim

Johnson, Albert

Lindsey, Leonard

Maher, John
Manworing, William H.
Maynard, Horace J.
Merritt, Franklin
Mitchell, Edward M.
Moore, William

Manworing, Samuel
Martin, William
Maynard, John
Miller, Charles F.
Monroe, Peter L.
Mowers, Thomas H.

Newton, Thomas R.

Nichols, Robert L.

O'Neil, Thomas

Parcell, Albert L.
Phelps, Edwin
Poole, John D.
Preston, James A.

Parsons, William A.
Pike, Elijah M.
Preston, George D.

Reed, Chauncey J.
Richard, Charles H.
Rowlingson, Theodore

Reed, John
Roome, Henry C.
Ruggles, Eli M.

Sackett, Addison L.
Shepard, George M.
Signor, George B.
Smullen, Edward
Southworth, William
Stevens, Samuel S.
Stockwell, Francis
Sturdavant, Eli
Surdam, Hiram

Shaver, John
Sherwood, Alonzo M.
Smith, Sidney M.
Southworth, Reuben
Springer, Barton
Stewart, Milton D.
Straton, Whitman
Surdam, John E.
Surgeant, Simon A.

Tucker, Bonaparte

Tyler, Nathan L.

VanDusen, John

VanVleet, William

Walker, Charles B.
Wasson, Clarence L.
Webb, John W.
Wightman, Oscar O.
Wilcox, David M.
Wood, John A.

Washburn, Wesley
Weaver, Charles
Wheeler, Ira H.
Wilbur, Stephen R.
Williams, Joseph H.

Company F

Aberle, Adam
Adams, William E.
Alden, Edward M.
Arnott, George C.
Atwater, William A.

Adams, John Q.
Alcott, James B.
Allen, James
Asley, John C. P.

Babrick, James
Bartholomew, Andrew J.
Bennett, Debois
Bixby, Lafayette
Bliss, Perry
Booth, Charles E.
Bowker, George W.
Britt, James
Brown, Parley M.
Brown, Robert
Burghardt, Francis

Baldwin, George H., Jr.
Benedict, William N.
Benson, William N.
Blackman, Samuel H.
Bly, Daniel
Bowes, John
Brewer, Seth E.
Brown, James
Brown, Robert
Bryan, Patrick

Carpenter, Theodore
Collins, James
Councilman, Truman
Covey, John M.
Culver, Lewis C.

Cleveland, Ezra
Cooley, Edward
Courtney, Charles I.
Culver, Daniel D.

Deery, Edward
Dibble, George W.
Dobie, William
Dyer, Jackson

Dewey, George J.
Dimick, Omer
Donegan, Patrick

English, George

Fenner, Frederick
Fiske, Charles
Fosgate, Blanchard M.
French, Charles H.

Figgs, Henry
Foot, Enos B.
Foster, John

Gardiner, William
Gray, Richard G.

Grammondz, Charles H.
Grey, Herman C.

Hall, Jerome

Hamilton, Christopher C.

Hamilton, Darwin H.
Harrington, Henry
Heady, Henry
Hicks, John P.
Holland, Charles H.
Homes, William J.
Horton, William H.
How, Jerome
Hughes, George

Handy, Melvin
Harrington, William
Heath, Sidney
Hogan, John J.
Holland, Harlam
Horton, Francis S.
How, Harvey L.
Howard, Gidian D.

Ingraham, Henry

Isenburg, George

Jefferd, Uriah H.
Johnson, Daniel

Jenbug, Elmorn
Johnson, Robert L.

Kennedy, George
Knapp, Ezra A.

King, Jacob

Lamb, Rodman
Lewis, Leonard
Lorringer, Josiah

Lewis, Dennis
Livermore, William B.

Makwith, William H.
McDonald, William D.
Mead, Gideon
Murray, John G.

Marvin, Seth
McGinness, Arthur
Monroe, Henry V.
Murray, Thomas

Nash, Martin M.
Nilsor, Karl
Northrup, James E.
Norton, Henry H.

Nicholis, George L.
Northrup, Isch W.
Norton, Asel H.

Oliver, Orville P.
Oliver, Simon

Oliver, Richard A.

Payne, Delos
Pierce, George F.
Pittsley, George W.
Puffer, Moses

Phelps, Harvey
Pierson, Peter H.
Pixley, Lorenzo

Reed, Almon L.
Rogers, Charles F.

Renseler, William C.
Rood, Giles O.

Rooks, Samuel

Saringer, Josiah
Self, William
Sheppard, Martin
Slade, George H.
Smith, Henry D.
Smith, Rufus C.
Stevens, Alla H.

Taft, Charles
Tewiliger, Barney
Toppins, John
Trafford, James H.
Tyler, Oliver

Schism, William H.
Sheppard, Alexander O.
Sherwood, George
Smith, George W.
Smith, John
Stephens, Eli
Stiles, Charles

Taft, Job
Tompkins, Elias B.
Trafford, Elias M.
Turner, Alpheus

Utter, William

VanBergen, George A.
Vanderburgh, James E.
VanIngen, Garrett

Walker, Robert
Wheeler, George A.
Wright, Edward G.

Yakel, Peter
Youngs, Frederick

Vandeburgh, Stephen P.
Vanderburgh, Stephen S.

Warne, Phineas H.
Williams, Emerson B.

Yarnes, Consider M.

Company G

Alden, Gillead S.
Atkins, James A.

Babcock, Edward A.
Ballard, James C.
Benjamin, Lathrop
Bird, Benjamin
Blatchley, Andrew A.
Blotchley, Charles
Buchanan, James H.

Andrews, Joseph E.
Ayers, Cavanaugh

Baker, Horace
Ballard, Sanford S.
Benn, Charles
Bird, Warren E.
Bloomer, Edward M.
Brown, Thomas
Bullock, William S.

Chase, Jarius S.
Crowfut, Charles K.

Cresson, Milton

Davenport, Frederick
Doolittle, Charles L.
Doolittle, Nelson E.
Draper, George W.

Dewey, Martin M.
Doolittle, Hervey I.
Doolittle, Stephen G.
Dusenbury, William

Edson, Daniel W.

Fairchild, Wiley
Frost, Merritt C.

Ford, Alvarado
Frost, Ransom H.

Garlic, Charles E.
Grodwant, Philip

Gilbert, Dewitt

Hailty, Gabriel F.
Haines, Hobart
Hallock, Ralph
Heath, Lewis B.
Hepesaul, Thomas
Hotchkiss, Leroy E.
Hulse, Gabriel C.
Hupman, Charles H.
Hupman, George S.

Haines, George W.
Hall, Robert H.
Hamilton, VanNess
Heath, Riley D.
Hoadly, Auburt
Howell, Isaac N.
Hunt, Amos C.
Hupman, Eli

Ives, Joshua

Judd, Jerome B.
Judd, Seymour L.

Judd, John D.

Kelmone, William H.
Kirby, James W.

Killmer, William F.
Knowlton, John

Marshall, William D.
Mayo, George
Moore, Levia E.
Moore, William O.
Morse, Milo E.
Morton, William E.

Master, William H.
Mayo, Willard
Moore, Whitney A.
Morse, Henry E.
Morse, Uri E.

Page, Whitney
Perkins, William
Piper, Hampton L.
Porter, Edward

Reed, Ichabod S.
Russell, John B.

Smith, Ezra P.
Smith, James
Spearbeck, Sandford L.
Springsteen, Robert
Stephens, Abisha
Swagart, Joseph W.

Tiel, Elmore
Tompkins, L. William
Twitchell, Samuel R.

VanNorwick, Isaac

Warner, George R.
Watrous, James E.
Welton, William H.
Whitney, Amos L.
Wooster, Uri T.

Parson, Simon A.
Piersall, Thomas H.
Plunkett, Franklin

Russell, Benjamin F.
Russell, Pliney A.

Smith, Franklin S.
Smith, Mason B.
Spring, Steuben
Springsteen, Urial
Stringham, Irving A.
Sweet, Calvin

Toby, John L.
Tompkins, Milton I.

Warner, Grover
Welton, Warren
White, Joseph E.
Wilds, John M.

Company H

Ames, James M.
Atwater, Ira G.

Bacon, Franklin
Bacon, Manly M.
Boakes, Frank
Brown, Jonathan

Carmon, Horatio
Carrier, James W.
Cassady, James
Cole, Chauncey H.

Amsbry, Charles H.

Bacon, Ichabod E.
Bacon, William A.
Boughton, Epenetus

Carnick, Henry O.
Carrier, Winfield
Clark, Lewis
Cole, Samuel C.
178

Collar, Moses W.
Corby, Samuel S.
Crawford, Lyman
Crowe, John

Corby, Israel L.
Cormack, Henry O.
Crocker, John H.

Daugherty, John W.
Davis, John Jr.
Davis, Lewis B.
Davis, Moses
Draines, Daniel D.
Dunning, John T.

Davis, Henry
Davis, Leroy
Davis, Mills
Demosthenese, Romine
Drum, William a.
Durfee, George C.

Edney, George
Edson, Seth
Eldridge, Clapper

Edson, James
Edwards, John P.

Flint, Jeremiah
Foster, Hiram F.

Flint, Lorenzo
French, William H.

Gardner, Harrison
Gates, William E.
Gray, George W.
Groves, James H.

Gates, Elwood F.
Ghoring, Henry L.
Gregg, Charles

Hakes, Ralsey W.
Hardy, Benjamin (born c. 1846)
Harper, Barton P.
Haxton, Abram
Hellmer, Thomas
Horton, James

Hardy, Benjamin (born c. 1841)
Hardy, Thomas
Hart, Gustave
Hayes, John
Holly, Lafayette

Jinks, Owin
Joiner, Henry K.

Johnson, Luther A.
June, James

Kain, Lawrence

Kilmer, Thomas

LaBarron, Asyl M.
Law, Albert
Lewis, Leonard
Livingston, Peter
Ludwig, Jacob P.

Ladue, George
Lee, Barney
Lewis, Wellington M.
Lockhard, William

Mack, Charles L.
Martin, George
McIntyre, Ezra
Meck, Charles L.
Morris, Almon
Morse, Justin
Murphee, John A.

Mahew, James M.
McCaslin, Albert
McNamara, Lewis
Moony, John
Morris, Oliver
Morse, Linus

Newton, George W.

Northrupt, William P.

Oliver, William
Osborn, William W.

Osborn, Joseph R.
Osburn, Benjamin

Palmer, Abile
Palmitier, Napoleon
Pingree, Augustus W.
Potter, Benjamin
Preston, Charles T.

Palmer, William R.
Perry, William H.
Pitts, Charles W.
Prentice, Charles H.

Quigley, Michael N.

Race, George
Riddle, Walter
Robins, John C.
Rosselle, Edward S.

Rhoades, David I.
Rider, Samuel
Rosselle, Benjamin E.

Sarine, John W.
Seeley, John H.
Slater, Israel
Smith, Jehial
Snook, William H.
Squairs, John

Scovel, Stephen M.
Shaw, Joseph C.
Sloat, Elijah
Sneeden, Moses
Snow, William H.
Stoots, John V.

Talmadge, David
Templar, Marshall E.
Terwilliger, George W.
Tuller, Charles
Tyler, James

Talmadge, William H.
Terwilliger, George
Tillotson, George W.
Tuttle, Theodore F.

Utter, William H.

VanGorden, Harris

VanName, John B.

Vermilyea, George W.
Verill, Joseph

Verill, George

Warner, Hoyt
Weaver, Dudley R.
Wilson, Aaron W.
Winters, Henry

Watson, John
Wem, Obadiah
Wilson, Henry J.
Woodburn, Clarence

Youngs, James E.

Company K

Aldrich, Henry
Atwell, Paul

Atwell, Elijah

Bagley, Edgar
Ball, Charles A.
Beaugare, Valentine
Bogardus, Charles A.
Braudski, Theoplis
Brown, Edward
Brown, John
Burt, Albert C.
Butler, Mathew M.

Baker, John
Barge, John
Bisbee, Noah
Bogart, Henry L.
Brown, Almiron
Brown, Edward M.
Burns, Edward
Burt, Franklin

Carl, Robert
Carr, John
Corbett, Timothy
Covert, Benjamin
Cronk, Charles
Crooker, Henry B.

Carmichael, Thomas
Conway, John
Covert, Abram
Crocker, Eli
Crooker, George F.
Cunningham, George

Debau, William
Donally, Thomas
Douglass, Charles
Dunham, Monrous L.

Decker, Jonathan
Donovan, Jeremiah
Dunham, Harrison C.

Eaglesfield, George
Edson, Seth

Eaglesfield, Wallace
Englis, George M.

Ferons, George W.

Ferrons, Lafayette

Fitch, Samuel A.
Florence, James
Fredenberg, William E.

Galloway, Stephen B.
Griffith, Isaac H.

Harding, Oliver P.
Harrin, Albert
Hayes, James
Heess, Reudolph
Hennessey, John
Hickey, John
Hoffman, George
Howard, Allison A.
Hughes, George C.
Hughs, Lafayette
Hurlburt, George

Johnson, Henry R.
Jordan, George

Kavannagh, Sylvester
Kincoid, John
Kity, William
Knight, Christopher

Lacy, Silas W.
Lawson, Charles E.
Lawson, Ezra (born c. 1848)
Love, Thomas

Martin, Daniel D.
Martin, William
McKee, John
Meaker, Andrew
Meaker, Nelson W.
Miller, Hebron E.
Miller, John P.
Moore, Isaac
Moore, Wilburt
Myers, William

Flecker, August
Foote, Henry
Frost, John

Granness, Marshall
Gryman, Reuban

Harmirn, Frank
Harris, Henry
Hayes, William
Heisler, Casper
Heutch, Lewis
Hinch, John
Holmes, William H.
Howard, Asa L.
Hughs, Isaac
Hull, Tompkins

Johnson, William H.

Kerr, James
King, William P.
Knapp, Job A.

Lawrence, Charles
Lawson, Ezra (born c. 1845)
Lee, John

Martin, Joseph P.
McAnamara, Patrick
McKune, Gilbert E.
Meaker, Hiram G.
Meaker, Oliver W.
Miller, John
Mills, Lymon S.
Moore, Samuel P.
Mott, Leroy

Nelson, H. S.

Patterson, George F. A.
Pencil, William N.
Place, William J.
Purnell, George W.

Ransom, Ambrose
Robinson, Leander S.
Ronkles, Charles F.
Ryan, John

Scofield, George
Sharp, William A.
Smyth, William F.
Strain, William
Swan, Charles

Tarbox, Charles L.
Taylor, James C.
Thurston, Frederick

VanHorn, George

Webb, William N.
Welch, Harvey
Wilkinson, Levi B.
Wilton, John T.

Zends, Erhardt

Nichols, Richard

Paul, John
Phinney, Martin V.
Procter, Albert D.

Reppold, Carl
Rochman, Egbert
Russell, Perry

Serry, Christopher
Simpson, Lewis L.
Stewart, William
Sullivan, John
Swift, Moses

Tarbox, George
Thompson, Joseph F.
Tremain, Frank W.

Welch, Ezeck
Wilbur, Henry H.
Williams, Monroe
Winters, Daniel c.

Appendix D - Compiled List of Men of the 89th Crossing the Rappahannock River, December 11, 1862

This list was compiled through the efforts of Captain Burt (Company K) after the end of the war. It seems to be the most accurate one ever compiled, since the original was never found.

Company A

Sergeants: George C. Hughes, John C. Kirtland, and Mordecai Williams

Corporals: Henry C. Adams and Henry E. Rowley

Privates: Irving Agney, Edwin O. Bennett, Robert Cannon, Charles Colton, Abram M. Creque, Edwin B. Curry, Edwin S. Kellogg, John H. Peck, Thomas Sarsfield, William Tailby, and Albert J. Turner

Company B

Captain: James Hazley

Corporal: David Harris

Privates: Joseph B. Bovee and Reed F. Francisco

Company C

Sergeants: Daniel R. Banford and William T. Eddy

Corporal: Avery Gardner

Company E

Corporals: Samuel F. Balcom, William Y. Clinton, and Whitman Stratton

Privates: Francis C. Barnes, Ransom E. Church, David P. Dailey, Mordicai Evans, Charles F. Everson, Rodney A. Harvey, Jay Lewis, Leonard G. Lindsey, Joseph Lorio, Robert L. Nichols, John D. Poole, Theodore Rowlason, Sidney W. Smith, Barton Springer, Samuel S. Stevens, William Van Vleet, Charles R. Walker and Charles K.

Weaver.

Company F

Corporals: Uriah A. Jeffries and Alex O. Sheppard

Privates: Nathan Fiske, George Isenburgh, Robert A. Oliver and Consider M. Yarns

Company G

Captain: Seymour Judd

Sergeants: William Dusenbury, Aubert D. Hoadley, William O. Moore, and Irving A. Stringham

Corporal: Riley A. Heath

Privates: Cavunough Ayrers, Charles Blatchley, James H. Buchanan, Charles L. Doolittle, Nelson E. Doolittle, George W. Draper, Ransom H. Frost, George W. Haines, Hobart Haines, Robert H. Hall, George Mayo, William H. Mayo, Whitney A. Moore, Simon A. Parsons, Sanford L. Sperbeck, Robert G. Springsteen, and James E. Watrous

Company H

First Lieutenant: Wellington Lewis

Sergeants: Samuel C. Cole, William H. French, Simon Springsteen, and Henry Talmadge

Corporal: George W. Tillotson

Privates: Ichabod E. Bacon and Matthew W. Snook

Company I

Privates: William J. Gilbert, George W. Hitchcock, William S. Law and William Scott

Company K

Captain: Frank Burt

Sergeants: Albert C. Burt and Marvin Watrous

Corporals: Noah Bisbee and George W. Ferous

Privates: Elijah Atwood, Edgar Bagley, Charles A. Ball, George F. Crooker, Henry B. Crooker, Abram Covert, George Englis, Isaac Hughs, George Hurlburt, Silas W. Lacy, Hiram G. Meaker, Gilbert A. McKune, William N. Pencil, Leander S. Robinson, Charles F. Runkles, Perry Russell, William Smyth, George L. Tarbox, Frederick Thurston, George W. Van Horne, and John T. Welton

Bibliography

Third Annual Report of the State Historian to the NYS Legislature, Albany, NY, 1897. Appendix D, pages 49-55.

New York Adjutant General's Office - Annual Report of the Adjutant-General, Register of New York Regiments in the War of the Rebellion, Albany, J. B. Lyon Co., 1902, Eighty-Ninth Infantry (No. 31), p. 172-341.

New York in the War of the Rebellion, 1861-1865, compiled by Frederick Phisterer, Albany, Weed and Parsons, 1890 Vol. 4, pages 2292-3003.

Records of Assistant Regimental Surgeon James Allen, for Company I, 1861-1864, p. 106.

Delaware Gazette, Delhi, NY. October 9, 1861, October 23, 1861, November 6, 1861, and June 29, 1864 issues.

Biographical Review - Leading Citizens of Delaware County, NY, Boston, Biographical Review Publishing Company, 1895, p. 60.

Soldiers Discharged, as recorded in the Delaware County Clerk's Office, Nos. 1, 2, and 3, 1861-1865.

Bloomville Mirror, Bloomville, NY. February 20, 1862, May 20, 1862, May 27, 1862, June 3, 1862, December 2, 1862, January 3, 1863, January 20, 1863, April 14, 1863, August 18, 1863, May 10, 1864, and October 18, 1864 issues.

Rochester Democrat and Chronicle January 26, 1901 issue.

Brevet Brigadier Generals in Blue, Roger D. Hunt and Jack R. Brown, 1990, Olde Soldier Books, Inc., Gaithersburg, MD, p. 199 – used with permission.

Official Records, War of the Rebellion, 1894, Washington, Government Printing Office. Volumes 9, 18, 19, 21, 25, 27, 28, 33, 35, 36, 40, 42, 46 and 51 in Series I, and Vol. 3 in Series II

Index

ALPINE, Mr. 41
ALVORD, Col. 98, 99
AMES, Adelbert (Gen.) 136
ANDERSON, R.H. (Gen.) 122, 139
ANDREWS, Joseph 124; M. 12; ___ 10
ATWATER, Elijah 137; William 144
AUSTIN, Sarah (Robinson) 85, 89, 90, 101, 105, 107, 112; William 85, 101
AVERY, George 69
BACON, Franklin 124
BAKER, Adolf 140
BARRICK, James 140
BARTHOLOMEW, Andrew 124
BEARS, Jim 81
BEAUREGARD, P.G.T.(Gen.) 134-136
BECKER, William 7
BEERS, William 124
BLINEBRY, Willard 86, 138
BOOTH, Charles 124
BOWKER, Hannah(Sackrider) 87, 89, 104, 105; William 105
BRATTON, John (Gen.) 138, 142
BRONSON, Burr 15
BROWN, Edward 140; Edward M. 140; Hiram 54, 86, 138; Solomon 124; Thomas 124
BUCKLEY, Michael 121
BURNHAM, Hiram (Gen.) 138, 139
BURNS, Edward 140
BURNSIDE, Ambrose (Gen.) 13, 27, 31, 33, 40, 95, 118, 119, 121, 123-130, 137
BURROWS, Alman 74
BURT, Albert 140; Franklin 127
BUTLER, Benjamin (Gen.) 133-136
BUTTS, Solomon 54, 86
CAHILL, William 121
CAMERON, Jehiel 124
CARMICHAEL, Thomas 140
CARRIER, Winfield 135
CASE, DAVID 28, 32, 47, 59; Mary 47, 59
CASSIDY, James 125
CHAMPION, S. B. 32, 68, 79, 94, 99
CLARK, Capt. 122
CLEMENS, John 133
COBB, Thomas (Gen.) 129
COLLINS, James 140
CONWAY, John 144
COOKE, J.R. (Gen.) 129; Sherman 125
CORBETT, Timothy 140
CORMACK, Robert 7, 17, 19, 22, 23, 27, 62, 67, 98, 106
COUCH, Darius (Gen.) 128
COURTNEY, Charles 124
COVERT, Abram 140
CRAFT, Benjamin 121
CRESSON, Milton 124
CRUMB, Samuel 72
CULLEN, Edgar (Col.) 139
DALY, Frances 140
DAVIDSON, John 68, 132
DAVIS, Harvery 133; Henry ; Jefferson (Pres.) 121; Moses 125

DEAN, Wilson 135
DEBAU, William 140
DEERY, Edward 140
DEWEY, Martin 124
DIBBLE, William 10, 72
DICKINSON, Daniel 117, 118
DIX, John (Gen.) 58
DIXON, David 29, 55, 58, 84, 88-90
DOUGLASS, A.B. 10; Charles 140
DRUMMOND, William 90, 106
DUMAS, David 140
DURAND, Charles 99
DURFEE, George 133
DYER, Jackson 135; Reuben 86
EAGLESFIELD, George 124
EARLY, Jubal (Gen.) 137
EARNEST, Clinton 130
EDSON, Daniel 124
EGGLESTON, Rev. 117
ELDRIDGE, Clapper 136
FLICK, ___ 82
EPPS, Henry 68, 106, 132, 138; Wesley 7, 11
ENGLAND, Henry 18, 19, 60; Theophilus 6, 8, 9, 11, 17, 18, 30, 37, 40, 55, 58, 60, 66, 67, 95, 132, 136
ENGLIS, George 144
ENGLISH, George 124
ESSLER, John 140
EUBANK, Capt. 123
EVERTS, Daniel 118
FAIRCHILD, Harrison 5, 24, 29, 31, 114, 115, 117, 118, 122, 127, 138, 139, 142, 143, 145, 146; Nancy (Stiles) 146; Philo 146

FIEBIG, Charles 27, 81
FIELD, Charles (Gen.) 138, 142
FISKE, Charles 132
FITCH, Butler 10; Samuel 137
FLORENCE, James 140
FOLMSBEE, George 138
FOOTE, Henry 138
FORREST, Nathaniel 124
FOSTER, Hiram 137; Robert (Gen.) 143
FRANCISCO, Henry 124
FRANKLIN, William (Gen.) 126, 128
FRENCH, William (Gen.) 128
FROST, John 140; Ransom 133
GALLOWAY, Stephen 125
GASTON, Anderson 90
GATES, Elwood 144
GETTY, George (Gen.) 75, 126, 128, 131, 132
GIBBON, John (Gen.) 143
GILBERT, Dewitt 124
GILLMORE, Quincy (Gen.) 134
GOODENOUGH, Nancy 4; Uriah 65, 78, 79
GORDON, John (Gen.) 143; S. 117
GRANT, Ulysses (Gen.) 133-135, 137, 142-144
GRAY, George 42; Richard 124
GREGG, General 138
GRODWANT, Philip 124
GROODY, Thomas 138
GROVES, James 136
GWYNNE, Sidney 121
HALSTEAD, William 6, 11, 15, 18, 20-23, 25, 27, 28, 29, 95

HANCOCK, Winfield (Gen.) 128, 134
HANFORD, Sheldon 35
HARE, Thomas 124
HARMIN, Frank 141
HARRIN, Albert 141
HARRINGTON, William 141
HARRIS, Averill 121; Henry 141
HART, Clinton 135
HATHAWAY, C. 117
HAWKINS, Rush 34, 119, 120, 126
HAZLEY, James 127
HEATH, Lewis 122
HECKMAN, Charles (Gen.) 138, 139
HELD, George 141
HEPESAUL, Thomas 135
HICKEY, John 141
HILL, A.P. (Gen.)124; D.H. (Gen.) 122
HINCH, John 141
HITCHCOCK, George 51
HOFFMAN, George 141
HOKE, Robert (Gen.) 142
HOLDEN, James 124
HOOD, John (Gen.) 137
HOOKER, Joseph (Gen.) 126
HOW, Harvey 138
HOWARD, Oliver (Gen.) 128
HUGHES, George 140; Patrick 42
HUMFREY, Willis 124, 130
HUNT, Aaron 11, 14, 79; ___ 10, 12, 23, 25, 26, 28-31, 39, 40, 43, 46, 47, 49, 59, 79
JACKSON, Thomas 128
JARDINE, Edward 122
JACOBS, Elder 64; Ira 17, 28, 32, 80, 82, 133
JARDINE, Maj. 122
JOHNSON, David 130
JOHNSTON, Joseph (Gen.) 142
JONES, Albert 106, 137; Alexis 42; David 123
JUDD, Seymour 127, 136
KAIN, Lawrence 135
KAVANNAGH, Sylvester 141
KEMPER, James (Gen.) 129
KING, Jacob 135
KITY, William 141
KNAPP, George 141
KNIGHT, Christopher 122
LAMB, Rodman 141
LAMSON, R.H. (Lt., USN) 131, 132
LANGLEY, ___ 91
LATOURNO, Joseph 141
LAW, Nathaniel 42; William 90, 135
LAWRENCE, Charles 141; Stephen 138
LEE, Dan 19, 21, 49, 54, 72, 115; Dominie 106; Robert E. (Gen.) 75, 76, 103, 121, 122, 125, 126, 128, 133-137, 143, 144; William Henry 76
LETTS, Delos 133
LEWIS, Wellington 127, 140
LINCOLN, Abraham (Pres.) 42, 51, 112, 117, 142, 143
LITTLE, James 101, 134
LONGSTREET, James (Gen.) 122, 123, 128-131, 138, 139, 142
LOOMIS, Charles 140
LOVGREN, Ed 18
LYBOLT, Albert 136
MACK, Charles 144
MAHEW, James 135

MAINS, Daniel 108, 138
MALLAN, James 137
MALLON, John 138
MANN, John 140
MANNING, Silas 136
MARTIN, John 141
MARTINDALE, John (Gen.) 134, 136
MASS, John 93; Mrs. 93
McCLELLAN, George (Gen.) 121-123, 125
McCONNELL, William 125
McDANIEL, Jenny 17
McGINNESS, Arthur 141
McINTOSH, ___ 123
McKEE, John 141
McKENZIE, James 65, 78, 80, 83, 87; Rhoda 82, 83, 107
McLAW, LaFayette (Gen.) 129
MEADE, George (Gen.)128, 133
MILLS, Lyman 124
MORGAN, Edwin (Gov.) 117
MOORE, Levia 122; Samuel 141; Whitney 132
MORSE, Linus 124; Uri 122
MYERS, Henry 141
MYRE, John 141
NEEDICK, Adam 124
NELSON, H.S. 141
NEWTON, George 141; Nathan 67
O'DONNELL, Jeremiah 17, 25, 42, 44, 57-60, 62, 63, 66, 72, 83
OLMSTEAD, S. 42
ORD, Edward (Gen.) 138
PAGE, Dr. 32
PATTERSON, George 141
PATZACK, Charles 141
PAYNE, Delos 136

PECK, Charles 136; John (Gen.) 130
PENFIELD, J. 12; ___ 10, 11, 13
PERKINS, William 124
PERRY, Russell 126
PETERS, John 91; Store 99
PICKETT, George (Gen.) 129, 139
PIERSALL, Thomas 124
PIERSON, Nathaniel 45, 118
PITTSLEY, George 136
PIXLEY, John 124; Lorenzo 141
PLUNKETT, Franklin 124
POOLE, John 138
POPE, John 121
PORTER, Edward 122
PUFFER, Moses 27, 28
PURNELL, George 141
RADIGAN, Jim 18
RAMSEY, David 144
RANSOM, Robert (Gen.) 129
REED, Almon 124; John 138
REILLY, Michael 141
RENO, Jesse (Gen.) 119, 120
RICHARDS, H. 30
RIFENBURY, William 86, 106
ROBIE, Jacob 118
ROBINSON, Alfred 3; Charles 4, 15, 22, 33, 71, 79, 92-94, 116; Daniel 4, 15, 22, 93, 94, 116; Dominie 106; Fannie 26, 44, 55, 66, 79, 82, 90, 96, 105, 109, 112; Lucy 116; Mary 1, 4, 5-16,18, 20-23, 26-34, 37, 39, 40, 42, 44, 45-53, 55-73, 77-89, 91-98, 100-106, 108-116; Mary (Slusser) 16, 26; Sarah 16, 28-31,

ROBINSON (Cont.) 37, 38, 45, 61, 63, 66, 69, 77; Sarah (Smith) 3, 10, 38, 43, 66, 71, 72, 79, 90; Thomas 10, 70, 96, 101, 104, 112, 116; William 1, 3, 5-17, 20, 22, 23, 26-34, 36, 37, 39, 40, 42-51, 53-73, 77-98, 100-107, 109-116
RODMAN, Isaac P. (Gen.) 122, 123
ROOME, Henry 138
ROSSELLE, Benjamin 136
ROSSITER, Edward 141
ROUNDY, Rev. 97
RULAPAUGH, Nicholas 124
RUSSELL, Pliney 136
RYAN, Patrick 141, 142
SACKRIDER, Daniel 28, 39, 42, 47, 56, 83, 91, 99, 111, 114; Hannah 21, 28, 42, 56, 66, 69, 71, 80, 83, 87, 89; James 91, 107; Lewis 52, 69, 79, 94, 105, 111, 114; Mary 4, 5; Nancy 4, 45, 52, 53, 56-58, 62, 64, 69, 82, 83, 107, 109; Timothy 4; William 105
SCHISM, William 144
SCOTT, Charles 140
SCOVEL, Stephen 124
SEYMOUR, Daniel 42
SHARP, William 141
SHEPARD, John 118
SHERIDAN, Philip (Gen.) 137
SHERMAN, William (Gen.) 137, 142, 143
SHERWOOD, George 124
SILLIMAN, Charles 90
SIMMONS, Al 74; James 63, 65

SIMONSON, Hiram 65
SLUSSER, Mary (Robinson) 16, 22, 64, 79, 96, 112; Wesley 22, 43, 55, 63, 65, 66, 72, 77, 85, 89, 90, 96, 103, 105, 113
SMITH, H. M. 46; Jehiel 132; John 141; Martin 39; Mason 137; Sarah 3, 10; Sgt. 140; William 118; William F. (Gen.) 135, 136; ___ 40, 46
SNOW, William 136
SOLOMON, Solomon 141
SPECHT, Joseph 141
SQUIRE, Truman 118
STANNARD, George (Gen.) 134, 136
STEPHENS, Abisha 137
STEWART, William 141
STILES, Charles 74; Nancy 146
STONE, Peter 141
STOTT, George W. 86, 90, 94
STRAIN, William 141
STRIBLING, Robert 132
STRINGHAM, George 141
STURGIS, Samuel (Gen.) 128
SULLIVAN, Patrick 121
SUMNER, Edwin (Gen.) 125, 126, 128, 129
SWAGART, Joseph 124
SWALLOW, Isaac 133
SWEET, John 133
TAYLOR, Robert 2
THOMAS, D. 92; David 141; Dewitt 65 Eugene 88, 89; George (Gen.) 137; Mrs. 88; Widow 91; ___ 94
THOMPSON, John 68, 132; Thomas 101, 134
TOMPKINS, Milton 124

TOOMBS, Robert (Gen.) 123, 124
TRAVER, Lucius 137
TREMAIN, Frank 144
TURNER, John (Gen.) 134
TWITCHWELL, Ira 106; Samuel 124
TYLER, Daniel (Gen.) 64
UTTER, William 132
VAN ANTWERP, Adelbert 124
VAN BUREN, Dean 130
VAN INGEN, Garrett 124
VERMILYEA, George 144
WAGNER, George 141
WALKER, Joseph 142
WASSON, Samuel 124
WATERS, Charles 41
WATROUS, James 133; Marvin 132
WEBSTER, Cornelius 118
WEED, Eliphalet 136
WEITZEL, Godfrey (Gen.) 139, 142
WHITE, John 41, 42; Joseph 138
WHITNEY, Boys 93; George 56; Mrs. 8, 29
WICK, William 124
WIGHT, James 86, 90-92, 94, 96, 99
WILLCOX, Orlando (Gen.) 126, 128
WILLIAMS, Electa 146; Harry 146; Monroe 133
WILSON, Henry 126; Lanora 124
WOOD, Stephen 42
WRIGHT, Col. 120
ZEH, Robert 9, 21, 42, 82
ZENDS, Erhardt 141

_____, Aunt Lib 21; Aunt Polly 65; Charles 63; Charley 18; Dan 17; Ebb 43; Gregory 102; James 104; Jane 17, 46, 58; Jane Ann 104; John 17, 25, 43; Mary 32; Meal 43; Olive 18

www.ingramcontent.com/pod-product-compliance
Lightning Source LLC
Chambersburg PA
CBHW071622170426
43195CB00038B/1776